Praise for Dr. Guy and *The Dissertation Warrior*

"Dr. Guy has an innate gift for breaking complex concepts and theories into practical and meaningful steps."

—Natalie Carter Johnson, Illinois, United States of America

"I could not have hoped for a bigger blessing on my PhD road than to have Dr. Guy at my side. His ultra-clear thinking saved me hours, if not a year, of work time."

—Yashoda, Berlin, Germany

"Speech is the mirror of the soul! It is a great pleasure to watch and listen to Dr. Guy's lectures. His advice comes from the bottom of his heart! Big thanks for your big heart!"

—Yerkhan Mindetbay, Kazakhstan

"Dr. Guy and his passion for the dissertation process creates within me a highly-confident spirit, which allowed me to embrace a seemingly arduous task with sustained motivation and aplomb from start to finish!"

—Leo Mora Jr., San Antonio, Texas, United States of America

"Dr. Guy provides insights in the PhD process that others can't!"

—Teresa J. Wilson, Sydney, Australia

"Dr. Guy is an excellent resource to help you navigate through and complete your dissertation! His tools are wonderful and give practical information to keep your dissertation organized."

—Cynde Wadley, Abilene, Texas, United States of America

"Dr. Guy has helped me answer the questions I didn't even know I needed to ask."

—*Delyth,* United Kingdom

"Providing the expertise and support that I felt was missing from interactions with my dissertation chair, department chair and school program, Dr. Guy has been the mentor and coach I desperately needed at a time when it felt I was wandering aimlessly in the wilderness."

—*Frank P. Mattero,* Fredericksburg, Virginia, United States of America.

"Dr. Guy has helped me in many ways in connection with my doctoral dissertation and in my motivation towards the process of becoming a PhD."

—*Stefan Kolimechkov,* London, United Kingdom

"Dr. Guy's book is a must have for all doctoral students who need help with starting a doctoral thesis or dissertation."

—*Erik Maldonado,* Barranquilla, Colombia

Dissertation Training Programs by Dr. Guy

The Dissertation Mentor® Accelerator Program

The Dissertation Mentor® Home Study Course

The Dissertation Mentor® One-To-One Mentorship

www.TheDissertationMentor.com

Other Books by Dr. Guy

Building the World's Greatest High School

Building the World's Greatest High School Workbook

Building the World's Greatest High School Student Leader

The Dissertation Warrior: *The Ultimate Guide to Being the Kind of Person Who Finishes a Doctoral Dissertation or Thesis*
Guy E. White, Ed.D.

This work is intended to give general information about the subject matters discussed herein. Laws, policies, and practices often vary from jurisdiction to jurisdiction, state to state, and school to school and are subject to change. All factual situations are different. Seek out advice for your individual situation. You, the reader, should consult with your own advisors regarding your individual circumstances. The author, publishers, and partners do not assume any responsibility for any errors or omissions. Also, the author, publishers, and partners specifically disclaim any liability resulting from the use or application of the information contained herein, and this work is not intended to serve as legal, professional, or academic advice for individual situations.

Published By:
Triumphant Heart International, Inc.
10117 SE Sunnyside Rd, F-403
Happy Valley, OR 97015
Get free training at www.TheDissertationMentor.com

Library of Congress Control Number: 2017910175
DMB_B1_170830

Cover design by Faceout Studio, Tim Green
Interior book design by Faceout Studio, Amanda Kreutzer
www.faceoutstudio.com

Illustrations by Bramanto Setyaki

THE
DISSERTATION
WARRIOR

The Ultimate Guide to Being the Kind of Person
Who Finishes a Doctoral Dissertation or Thesis

GUY E. WHITE, ED.D.

To the Dissertation Warrior: Dare.

TABLE OF CONTENTS

NOTE FROM THE AUTHOR

Creativity, getting what only I could create into this world, is not my passion;

it's my religion.

CONTROVERSY

When I was four years old, I learned how to time travel. My mother, who was (perhaps overly) concerned with ensuring that I would become an upstanding citizen in the world, would have me complete worksheets and various reading and writing exercises most days before playtime. At this age, all I wanted to do was play — sitting there doing an academic exercise that I was not particularly interested in felt like eating salad. Visually, even now as I type this, I can remember her face and her wagging finger as she said, "If you quickly complete your work, you'll be able to go out and play." Although she did not intend to, she implanted programming that, to this day, has become one of the grandest gifts of my lifetime: the ability to see what needs to get done, the capacity to intuitively know how to get it done, and the fortitude to sit and finish with my monumental power of focus. I also learned very quickly that when something demanding my attention was the path to get where I wanted to go, 99% of everything else simply did not matter. So, if I had to write out the letter "A" six times to go outside and play, it no longer mattered that my younger brother had stolen my favorite toy, that the cat was provoking my attention outside the screen door, or that fish-stick dinner smelled really good — all my attention was pouring into finishing. Almost nothing else mattered. When you live your entire life like 99% of things don't really matter, save only those things that are getting you where heaven wants you to go, that's time travel.

I cringe when I do my nightly "scroll" through Facebook® and see so many people harping about politicians, spending so much time capturing imaginary monsters, and liking photos of other people living out their dream lives when they themselves do not spend enough time pursuing their own happiness. Why give so much attention to the things that simply do not matter in comparison to your dreams? Why is it so common that students will spend hours answering mundane request after request via email at their places of employment but not set aside the time required to complete those special activities that will contribute to long-term happiness? In my vocation, I've interacted with thousands of doctoral students, and nearly all of them pursue this degree because they believe they have a calling they are answering. They are pursuing their ultimate calling in life. That feels like a big freakin' deal to me! Why, then, is their dissertation, their path to finishing their doctoral journey, the last thing that typically gets attention in their schedules? If God arrived in my office right now and said, "Dude, you need to finish this book manuscript within the next month," 99% of everything else in my life would probably have little or no need for attention — not really. Yet one of my recent surveys to students inside The Dissertation Mentor® Accelerator Program revealed that more than half of them felt that it was the will of a higher power (however they defined that) for them to finish their dissertation. I wonder if they think about that when they are planning their daily calendar. Would God's will get first slot? Ten minutes after lunch? A couple hours on the weekend? Even if students don't feel it's the divine's calling to finish their dissertation, they feel the weight of this project — that something in life would be wrong, unfinished, and disappointing if they never finished this thing. Why, for so many students, does the dissertation become one of the last things that gets time in their lives? When you realize that for you, sitting there and writing your dissertation is the path to happiness and more fulfillment (if not the calling of God himself), so much of everything else becomes unimportant and cringe-worthy.

This view of my universe, of which you and I are part, is a controversial one. Most people don't enjoy it when others critique them on their use of time. Also, believe it or not, some university professors don't like even the hint of the idea that writing a dissertation could be done more effectively and quickly. Also controversial is my calling out of so many hucksters on the Internet who are robbing students worldwide by promising "editing" services wherein one is handed a "finished" dissertation — a quick road to shame and expulsion, for sure. For these reasons, I need to make sure you know what I stand for. This way, you can make the decision of whether or not this book should be returned to Amazon.com or wherever you found it. Here are my values relating to writing your dissertation:

1. There are no quick fixes. Dissertations require significant investments of time and consistent effort. This is not a "finish fast" book — this is a "finish better" book. It could take you years to finish. We better get moving!

2. Your chair or principal advisor is your partner in this process, even if you don't always feel that way! This book will provide you with some ways of looking at your dissertation work that won't necessarily always be consistent with your chair's coaching; always trust your advisor. This person is your chief ally.

3. The dissertation process can be broken down into manageable steps — you simply need to know those steps and undertake them. Though not everyone must use the same methods, there are some strategies that are more wisely implemented than others. This book will show you what I think is most wise.

4. My way is *not* the only way. This book is about showing you my perspective; it's not the only perspective. I'm not always right. I don't know it all. Many people know much more than I do! This book is not peer edited or "scholarly" in the sense that other books on the subject of dissertation writing are. This book, regardless, will bless you.

If you're still with me, and I hope you are, put on your helmet and let's begin.

PHILOSOPHY

In this section, I talk about the mind frames that create doctoral graduates.
I also destroy the ways of seeing the dissertation process that probably will
prevent you from ever finishing.

01

YOU HAVE TIME TO READ THIS BOOK

What are your top three priorities in life today? Seriously, say them out loud, or maybe say them slightly under your breath so you don't scare the people around you. STOP and do this please. PERFECT.

Now, what got most of your time so far today? Chances are that what got your time today was everything else. Sure, your spouse and family are probably number one, but they did not get your first energy today. Yes, your love of God or your own personal development is important to you, but you may not be among the small percentage of persons in the world who sat to pray or hit the gym just after sunrise this morning. Chances are, you are like most individuals who simply got up, got dressed, got to work, and happened to get to reading this book at some point today. Our priorities don't always mesh with our schedules, unless dire things happen. It's often when our world seems to be falling apart that our priorities fall in line with our schedules.

This past April, my stomach decided to play a trick on me. Apparently, all the coffee, lemonade, and spicy food that I enjoyed consuming eroded part of my stomach lining. There were a few days that were quite scary. I could not eat anything, and doctors were doing frightening tests on my liver, gallbladder, and other parts of my body to determine if anything more serious was going on. I was losing lots of weight fast. A small life crisis seemed to emerge from all of this. I realized that my schedule and my priorities were not completely aligned, and this imbalance helped create this uneasy health situation. Suddenly, I found myself meditating in the mornings again. I was reading literature and listening to soothing music. I was more mindful of the food that was going into my body and the effects it could have on my soma. I was slower and more patient with others. I was more forgiving and understanding of my own personal limitations. For about six weeks, my whole life was completely upended, and it was glorious, frightening, and holy. During this time of personal upheaval, not the first that's happened in my life, I was reminded of the importance of giving my first energy to those things that mattered most to me — because in the end, when my body was under ominous threat from a possible unnamed catastrophe, I realized time is quite short. My personal hope is that you will not need a mini-life or real-life crisis to wake you up. My prayer, as I write this thing, is that you get to do that without the massive heartache and heartbreak. That's why I'm writing this thing: to help you get what you want and have peace.

You have time to read this book. Today, billions of people will be giving dozens of minutes, if not hours, to browsing their favorite social media platforms. They won't create a thing in the process; they are only drinking up the information being put out by others. Millions, if not billions, will binge-watch their favorite shows. They will listen to the same popcorn-quality music on the way to work that they listen to most days. Yet if today was one of the finite number of grains of sand in an hourglass mounted to their foreheads, they probably would interact with their time quite differently. When I was writing my own dissertation, I was a public school teacher with the entire summer off. Bravely, I sat down every day to write this thing...only to find myself playing Legend of Zelda for hours at a time. One day, I realized that if I never finished this thing, I could point to my gaming system, my phone, and a host of other seemingly unimportant time-drains in my life and say, "I gave up my doctorate to play video games." The thought made me sick to my stomach, and I finished a year later. Today, what are you giving up your doctorate for? Is it worth it? I met a guy today who is battling life-threatening cancer, but he said, "I will finish this dissertation if it's the last thing I do." He's serious. In your priorities, where does this dissertation thing stack up? Most people would put it right under family, God, and job. But is that where it ends up in the schedule?

Personally, I don't see this doctorate thing as another niche on your résumé or vita; I see it as a road to personal, professional, and spiritual transformation. Sorry to get all "woo woo" spiritual on you, but I really believe that your decision to go to school for another three to six (or more) years had a lot more to it than promotion and higher pay. Getting a doctorate smacks of personal destiny to me — as if you have a purpose in the world, and this is one of the ways that you thought you could go about fulfilling that purpose. That puts a lot of fire in my furnace over here on this end of the keyboard, as this book and I can help you get to that destiny. I take that very seriously; do you? Once, I had a yoga instructor say to me, point blank, "If I said that this practice could extend your life by a dozen years, would you come do this every day?" My answer was clearly "yes!" So, I turn this logic back on you: If I told you that this book could help you be more able to fulfill your personal, professional, and spiritual destiny, would you read one chapter every day? My hope is that the answer is "yes." If not, and if you don't find the next few chapters helpful, please return this book to where you bought it or hand it to someone else. You have time to read this book because getting your doctoral degree by finishing your dissertation is one of the chief callings of your life; you would not have entered this doctoral program if it were not already a calling within you. So, answer the calling and read this book. You have the time. The only time you have to finish this dissertation is now. Everything beyond now is simply a hope. Get to work.

02

HOW YOU DO IN ONE, YOU DO IN ALL

The evening before the beginning of my fourth-grade year at school, I boxed up many of my toys from my "youth" that were no longer needed, vacuumed my room, set out my clothes for the following day, and created a handwritten schedule that I posted on my wall next to my door:

> › "7:00 a.m. – Wake;
> › 7:15 a.m. – Drink glass of milk and have toast;
> › 7:25 a.m. – Walk to the bus stop…"

The list went on. The next morning, I put on my neon green t-shirt and walked the 30 feet from my door to the bus stop, which was in my front driveway. The first day of school was a long-anticipated and greatly longed-for ritual that marked the passage for my eight-year-old self into some semblance of adulthood — I got to play on the big kids' playground this year, after all!

I tell you all of this to simply illustrate a part of my character that has been in place as long as I can remember: New beginnings, new eras of life are very exciting to me, and I take great steps to make such threshold moments into elaborate rituals. I carry that part of my character with me everywhere I go. I'm always on the lookout for the quickest way to reach the pinnacle of accomplishment in whatever "era" of life I am working through so that I can experience the fresh feeling of entering a new one. This is hugely influenced by my cultural upbringing in my family, religion, and nation; I'm always looking for the next step. This seeps into every bit of my work ethic; my way of being as a friend, lover, and father; and my ways of going about my daily life. I don't leave my character at the door every day; I carry it through every aspect of my life — for good and for bad.

My impatience to finish and move on is always felt.

My inability to slow down and be fully present in the moment is one of the greatest challenges of my life.

I'm constantly motivated for progress and find myself quickly losing energy if progress is not quickly felt.

No matter what I am doing, whether writing a paper or this book, being a father, teaching, washing my car, or considering purchasing a new iPhone, these aspects of my character come with me.

How I do in one thing, I do in all things. Who I am in one thing is who I am in all things.

How you do in one thing, you do in all things. Whether you are writing a dissertation, being a spouse (or ex-spouse), doing your work to earn a paycheck, or shopping for groceries, you are the same person everywhere you go. Even when you are putting on your student hat and sitting down at your keyboard to write the paper that will allow you to finish this doctoral journey, you are still the same person you were earlier today, last night, a week ago, probably wearing dozens and dozens of hats in the process.

When I work with doctoral students, they are obsessed with learning the methods, tips, processes, and "hacks" in regard to writing that will allow them to finish faster. They want me to tell them how to write a problem statement, how to create logical alignment in their draft, how to get out of the weeds when writing their literature review, and how to choose the right methodology for their study. What they often fail to realize is that all of these concerns are secondary to becoming the *type of person* who could finish a dissertation in the first place. If you do not have the character of a person who finishes a dissertation, what is the likelihood that you will finish a dissertation? It's like expecting a person who does not have the character of a bodybuilder to win the Mr. Universe® competition. Your personal character is your strongest asset and, potentially, your most taxing liability.

When you are sitting down to do your writing, you are not simply a writer —

you are YOU doing the writing. The emails that have been mounting, that mess that has been piling up at home, the emotional angst felt with loved ones, the bills — everything is following you into that writing experience. Most importantly, your way of working with those things is following you into the writing too. If you are the type of person who has very little time for your family in your life, I have a sinking suspicion that you also might be the type of person who has very little time for your dissertation. Conversely, if you are the kind of person who thrives in chaos, the step-by-step, slow, incremental process of writing a dissertation could be quite taxing. Each year, I work with thousands of doctoral students through my videos and online offerings, and some I work with in close-knit classroom settings. When I work closely with students, I see how they approach their university studies, and the way they have approached the majority of their assignments is how they work in their dissertation world. Last-minute assignment writers seem to typically behave as last-minute dissertation writers.

If you feel that your dissertation writing has not gone as planned, that you are not on the schedule that you desire, and that you have not received the results you expected, then it's time to look at THE WAY you are approaching your dissertation writing IN LIFE. This book is packed with many writing tips, but until you are the type of person who can use them, they will be useless. To change your writing, you may have to change your character.

03

LITTLE DRAGONS VS. BIG DRAGONS

I taught high school for the first 12 years of my life as an educator, packing 35 teenagers of various physical configurations into a small room on the suburban campus at which I was a student. Walking down those bubble-gum-littered hallways as a 25-, 30-, 35-year-old teacher, only a handful of years after I had graduated, I constantly drank from the firehose of nostalgia supported by sights, sounds, and smells of being young: remembering my first kiss, the day I found out I was not accepted to my top-choice schools, and the days of walking through the hallways trying to not look lonely. I am constantly reminded how being a teenager was so hard, but I have the hindsight today to know that it truly was not THAT hard, given what I know now. This paradox, of sorts, intrigues me: How can we fall for the trick, time and time again, that the little dragons in our lives are the fiercest foes that deserve our energies? How can we constantly miss the big dragons lurking out there in the darkness? I fall for this trick every time.

The little dragons that I'm fighting today are a lack of sleep, my children's head colds, and the interview for the faculty job that I had earlier this week. Right now, these are the things I'm losing sleep over. (What a funny thing to lose sleep over — not having enough sleep.) In regard to your dissertation, you may be worried about the emails that are piling up in your inbox, the boss who is expecting you to get more work done in less time for no more pay, and making sure that your dissertation chair is happy. These are the little dragons — problems that are in the foreground of your life. They move fast and get lots of attention; THEY LOVE

YOUR ATTENTION. They are attempting to distract you; don't fall for it. One day, you will wake up and realize, "Wow, that was not as bad as I thought it was at the time. I'm better for what happened. I'm stronger now for all that happened." You need not defer life's wisdom till the end. You could pick up this wisdom today: Little dragons come and go; they have no teeth — not really.

Big dragons have teeth. And truly, one of these big dragons will destroy you one day. A year ago, I was in a room of doctoral students in Orange County, California, when one bombastic, macho-presenting dude stood up in the middle of my talk (fortunately, it was during the question-and-answer phase) and said, "For all the motivation I have been given over the years, nothing has stuck — nothing has motivated me. What can you say that will motivate me to finish this thing?"

I'll tell you what I told him: "One day, you will die."

Death is the big dragon that every single person reading this text will have to meet one day. No one gets to avoid it, unless, that is, you are caught up in the Rapture or the Singularity or something. Time is ticking away, and there will come a time when writing your dissertation is no longer possible. Already, writing your dissertation may be slipping into a world of time where it is no longer probable. Ten years from now, five years from now, three years from now, do you truly believe that you'd be willing or able to finish this thing?

I have three main motivations in my life. Motivation number three in my brain is "Don't make regrets." This differs from its more popular rock-star cousin, "No regrets." When I personally commit to "don't make regrets," what I am really saying is, "One day, dude, you're going to be an old man who still has to look at himself in the mirror for the remainder of his life. One day, you're going to be on your deathbed and losing your faculties to communicate. One day, dude, you're no longer going to be pursuing your 'life's work' in the way that you are trying to today. Do you want to have anything hanging over your head when you find yourself in such a position? You don't even know when that might happen. Time is short, so get moving." You never know when this biggest of dragons is going to show up in your life; do you want to have regrets present when he does? For all that is good in this world, I want to have nothing to do with regret when my time on this earth ends — and I'm willing to work harder than I ever have in my life to make sure that I get to leave this planet with a clear conscience.

On my deathbed, I will be a man who can look back over the course of his whole life and say, "That was not so bad. Those things that I obsessed about when I was 13, 33, 53, and so on were not as challenging as I thought." Speak to old people, and they'll tell you the same thing. They'll tell you that failure is not the same as regret. They'll say that when you fail, you learn, but when you give up, you'll regret. Talk to old folks in elderly homes — they don't obsess about failures; they are haunted by regret.

Borrow from tomorrow's wisdom today: One day, you will be mentally walking through the hallways of your past, long after all the crises, emails, and hours and hours of typing. When you walk those hallways, what will you find there?

04

DISCARD WHAT'S UNHELPFUL

From a very young age, I've used cleaning as a mix of coping mechanism and moving meditation. When my hamster died, I cleaned out his cage, scrubbed it down, tightly packed its contents in wrapping, and nestled it into a newly formed space in my closet. I vacuumed the room for an hour, swept out the edges of the floorboards, and made clean lines in the carpet as if my room was one of those lawns from those mansions in television shows. When I failed my first attempt at my behind-the-wheel exam for my driver's license, I retreated to the same bedroom of my childhood and packed up everything from my "younger years," which apparently had ended about 45 minutes prior, threw out everything superfluous, and journaled my 10 steps to get the heck out of my home town — I was fed up. Even today, as I write this, my wife and I are planning a move out of state, a change of career paths, and a whole new way of living with our children and community; we found ourselves packing up all the no-longer-used baby gear to be given away to anyone in need. Often, for new things to come into our lives, we have to make space for them. Always, those things that are in our lives, for good or for bad, impact the way we can carry out our work. Sometimes, we are carrying so much that our personal situation can begin to feel unworkable.

You are ambitious. Of all the things in the world, you took on a doctoral degree. You could have learned tennis, become a professional poker player, or decided that the years of work were not worth it, opting for vacations twice a quarter instead. By the nature of this ambition, my suspicion is that you have taken on much in your life. You probably have a demanding career or job. You probably have time- and energy-consuming relationships with many others in your life. Chances are, your email inbox is filled to the brim with other people's priorities bearing down on you. As you were building your career and your education, you took on all that you felt was in concert with your desires for the future. Now, you are trying to finish this dissertation, and it feels like it all is too much. I want you to hear the message that your soul is probably sending you: "This is too much for you to handle." Sounds taboo, right? It almost feels like it's sacrilege to say such a thing out loud. For you, this phrase may smack of defeat. But you do feel overwhelmed, don't you? Fortunately, this is not a message warning of defeat. After speaking to hundreds of doctoral candidates over the past three years, I can tell you this for sure: These moments of hardship are hints that a transformation is happening. You are transforming, and this doctoral journey is part of the path of this transformation.

Often, people crave a grand escape. They envision themselves making secret preparations for an entire change of life, and when fully ready to depart, they imagine making an equally climactic exit from their weighty jobs, relationships, gym memberships, and the like. Most of the time, doctoral candidates act as if one day they will be done with their doctoral degree, graduate, find a promotion or new venture, and move on to the next era in their lives. Their vision is clean, emotionally edifying, and adventurous — like packing up all of your wanted belongings and moving a state away. Most doctoral candidates want this era of their lives to end and to be able to move on. Are you ready to move on?

The doctoral journey is not a clean one. It can often feel like you are trying to move forward, being held strongly by the legs and by the hands of all the forces in your life that won't let you move as quickly as you desire. Instead of catching these forces by surprise one day and saying, "In two weeks, I'm quitting and moving to the forest to find happiness," you have to slowly pry each finger apart to lessen their grips on you, you have to cajole and negotiate with others to let go while even others swear they will never let you go — all of this while writing a 200+ page paper. You don't get to wait until graduation day to begin the process of letting go and moving on; you have to start that transformation today.

Regardless of the weight you are currently carrying, your situation is still workable. Until the moment of your last breath on this planet, you will always have the chance to better your situation, wherever you are. Today, you will not graduate. Today, you will not finish your dissertation. Today, you will not be able to move on to that new position, venture, or horizon that you are deeply craving. However, today you can take one step in that direction. You can discard what is unhelpful in your life. You can slowly, very slowly, lessen your personal commitments, begin clearing out that inbox, box up cluttering aspects of your life and give them away. Today, you can take stock of those people and organizations in your life that have expectations of you. Today, you can decide which of these need to be phased out within the next three, six, and 12 months. Today, you can break out your day calendar, log each and every action you take during the day, and sit down (perhaps with a glass of wine) in the evening to decide what daily behaviors are no longer serving you. And even if none of this is possible, you can still let go of the habit of closing your day with television, opting instead for sitting for just three minutes in silence with yourself, breathing deeply. In those moments of silence in the late evening, when you are often too afraid to spend a couple moments alone with yourself, you may think that everything in your life is falling apart. Remember, this transformation, called a "doctorate," that you have signed up for includes leaving something behind. Gently discard what's no longer serving you.

05

IDEAS MEAN NOTHING

So much of Western culture is built on the idea that something is missing from our lives. Walk through a shopping mall, spend 60 seconds on your favorite social media app, or go old school and watch some television, and you'll see a catalog of wanting. There is always going to be someone out there who is trying to peddle to you the notion that you are lacking. With the exception of some lifelong Buddhist monks and other holy practitioners I've encountered, I have never met anyone who has not succumbed to the temptation of buying something unnecessary. The paradox, of course, is that nothing bought can make us complete. Worse yet, there is something extra interesting about the human compulsion to purchase something and use it once or twice, only to do nothing with it in the future. Buy that exercise bike. Buy that gym membership. Buy those university courses. Then, not much happens after that. Once-used items in our lives litter our physical and mental worlds like a collection of shiny new ships wrecked on a resort beach; the idea of doing things is far more attractive than the act of doing them.

As a dissertation chair, I have received dozens of emails from candidates saying, "I'll have these first three chapters to you by X date." Much of the time, that date comes and goes without the deliverable in my hands. In The Dissertation Mentor® Accelerator Program and Home Study Course, I highlight how making long-term promises to ourselves and others is often one of the brain's clever tricks to not getting any work done at all. A long-term goal easily becomes simply a goal deferred. It's like being a yoga practitioner: You don't become one by owning an expensive mat, having a membership somewhere, or wearing awkwardly tight-fitting clothing and beads. You *are* a yoga practitioner every time you actually land on your yoga mat, engage in the practice, and then draw that practice out into your world. Similarly, you are not a doctoral student because you are enrolled in continuation courses through your university, communicating with your chair every few weeks or so, or because you have an anticipated graduation date of year 20-whatever. You *are* a doctoral student when you actually are gliding your highlighter across a page, digging into your favorite research database, or clicking away at your keyboard. Ideas about when you'll finish mean nothing. The actual practice and execution of finishing is what matters — and where there is an actual possibility of transforming your life.

As a side note of commentary, I'm of the opinion that professors like myself are guilty of being co-conspirators in unproductive writing behaviors. As teachers, it's natural for us to want to provide deadlines, help create three-month action plans, and help provide accountability toward those deadlines. As coaches who may only interact with you a handful of times between now and that looming deadline out there, I'm sure many of us think that we have done you a service by asking you to pin down a date and attempting to hold you to that. In my experience, though — and I admit that this may not be the experience of every professor — I've found that deadlines like this in doctoral work potentially hinder candidates. As you can gather by this chapter of this text, I'm of the belief that your focus and my focus should be for you to perform a set practice *each day* of reading, annotating, and writing. That's it. Without that daily practice, progress will NOT manifest. If you are not writing your dissertation, then *you are not writing your dissertation*. I'm still perplexed each time I hear a friend say to another, "I go to the gym," leaving out the fact that he has not been to the gym in three weeks. After how long of not going to the gym are you *no longer* a gym-goer? By comparison, I often hear doctoral candidates say, "I'm in the process of writing my dissertation." Still, after how long of *not writing* your dissertation are you still considered to be "a dissertation writer"? What makes you a dissertation writer is that you are actually doing the tasks, each day or so, in concert with writing your dissertation. If a couple weeks go by and, not due to personal tragedy, you have not done any of the tasks that will help you bring a dissertation into the world, you are probably more of a dissertation hobbyist than a dissertation writer. A person who goes to a golf course every month or two is not a pro golfer. Similarly, how can a doctoral student expect to climb to the pinnacle of academic degrees and not behave like a "pro" in training. Deadlines will always exist, but they are not the point — focus on gliding your eyes across some pages of research each day, taking some notes about what you read, and clicking those fingers on your keyboard, adding to the hundreds of pages that will make up your final paper.

Your future is an idea. Those doctoral-degree-driven job promotions, those celebratory vacations, and even graduation is not yet real. None of these things will come to be until you personally stop ideating about them and actually do the tasks in concert with making those things happen in your life. At some point in the future, you will either have a graduation or have a large school bill not connected with a degree. Which one do you want to be holding? It's like two people waking up in the morning: One wants "to be happy one day in the future"; the other wants "to be happy today." Which one would you rather be? Fortunately, you have a choice. If it is early enough in the day right now, put this book down, go print an article, and get reading. If you are reading this close to slumber-time, then set your alarm back only 30 minutes to begin your day by executing on *being* a doctoral student.

06

EVEREST. OLYMPICS.

When I was 23 years old, I worked for a popular casual dining restaurant chain in the United States. It was my first full-time job after my undergraduate studies, and I was paying off all the mistakes of my college years: supporting ex-girlfriends and buying anime DVDs, all on high-interest credit card debt. I wanted to join the Peace Corps, but they did not let anyone with credit card debt into the service. So I sold much of what I owned, moved in with a 78-year-old mentor for $15 monthly rent, and worked a seven-hour substitute teaching job in the morning and a 10-hour restaurant shift in the evening. This is what was required to achieve my dream of going to Nepal to teach kids English. So, when my boss's boss came to me to inform me that I was required to take my yearly vacation hours, I was devastated. "James, I can't afford to go on vacation." "Guy," he gave a puzzled frown, "we pay for you to go on vacation." Six hours later, I went to my 10-foot-by-10-foot rented room, opened a dusty box, took out a globe of planet Earth, gave it a spin, and my finger landed on Peru. An hour later, I booked a two-week Peruvian vacation, including a three-day walk in the Inca Trail to Machu Picchu.

A few days later, I received a FedEx® package with my welcome packet from the tour company. I'll never forget the alarming yellow piece of paper in there that had the title "Warning!" Reading carefully, I slowly realized, line by line, that I had signed up for a highly physically demanding hike. The packet described steep steps, huge elevation gains, and multiple ecological zones, including the possibility of snow. "You should come accustomed to hiking in elevated terrain for approximately 10 miles each day," the paper read. Attached was a recommended hiking schedule. By the time I reached Peru, I had done *none* of the training. As Freddie, our guide, began strapping an oxygen tank to his back, I realized the seriousness of the situation. I was the most unfit man on this hike. I was considered more high risk than some of the elderly hikers who looked like bodybuilders trapped inside a loose bag of leathery skin. "I could die on this hike," I kept thinking; this was not helpful. Needless to say, I made it through alive. Mind you, many porters deserve the credit for this, as they carried my things and sometimes helped me just take one more step. I should have never been on that trail. I treated it like a vacation or hobby. This experience was quite profound for me. I began to think about how those who prepare for the Olympics or an Everest climb could *never* treat such a feat with anything less than the respect of something so rare, so exclusive. Those who dare to do that which only 1% of persons on the planet will ever do have my highest respect.

You are just like an Everest climber or an Olympian. No one — *no one* — finishes their dissertation as a hobbyist. No one dabbles in doctoral studies in such a way that culminates in a dissertation, defense, and graduation — no one! By taking up this task, you have said, "I am attempting to be one of those few people on the planet who will ever accomplish this highest of academic honors." Do you, then, treat this endeavor with the same level of respect and calculation as an Everest climber who will risk his life to climb that mountain, or an Olympian who will shape her entire life around the pursuit of bodily perfection? Just as an Olympian trains each and every day, are you orienting your life around your dissertation with the same level of commitment and regard? You cannot be extraordinary without doing extraordinary things; you cannot be the exception without acting exceptional. Of all the things you could have done in the world, you decided to pursue a doctoral degree. Accordingly, will you back up this decision with the actions that will allow for you to complete this momentous accomplishment?

Think of the qualities of exceptional people doing exceptional things in the world. Everest climbers will train for years on end through smaller to larger and larger physically breaking tasks. They will push their bodies to the limits of what they think is possible in an effort to establish new baselines for their daily, sometimes automated, behaviors. They will come to a point where hiking dozens of miles is child's play. They will learn to function with less sleep. They will learn how food impacts their physiology, including their mental clarity. They will have to master their time in service of their aims. Everything in their lives enters the service of their ultimate goal. Would it be possible to approach your work in the same way? If you truly believe it is your calling on this planet to finish this degree and enter a new era of life wherein you will most likely do the work for which you were placed on this planet, would you be willing to take drastic measures to make this possible? Would you be willing to redefine your relationship to social media, television, food, music, negative talk, family, caffeine, alcohol, rest, sleep, routine, time, and anything else in your life that could be of service or be a hindrance in your sole aim of meeting your destiny by finally finishing this paper?

Like any person looking to perform a feat of such rarity, there is a timeframe in which it is possible. There are far more young Olympians than there are old! This may be the golden age of your life in which it is possible for you to make the adjustments required to fulfill this truly rare accomplishment. Each day, as you contemplate your dissertation work, ask yourself, "Am I a Dissertation Warrior, or a dissertation hobbyist?" Truly, I hope you take up the warrior's calling! Each day, the choice is yours!

———————————————————————

07

PEOPLE LOVE THAT YOU'RE ON A DIET
UNTIL YOU EAT AT THEIR HOUSE

In my experience, people love the idea of exceptionality far more than the execution of exceptionality. We love the idea of people losing unhealthy weight, gaining heart strength, and eating well, until their actions cause us to make adjustments to our lives. To illustrate this, go to any family dinner around a holiday and quietly attempt to abstain from one of the main or side dishes for the sake of health. Quietly pass the mashed potatoes or bread to the next person without partaking, and you may be the recipient of snide remarks, questions, and the type of glaring only disapproving aunts can provide. People love that you are on a diet until you are eating at their dinner table.

This is exactly how many people view your dissertation work and your doctoral studies. They love the idea of you writing your dissertation. They love the idea of you graduating. They love the idea of you being well, being happy, and being more able to do your calling in the world. They love the idea of you being done with school (finally). However, tell them that you won't be able to make the regular family get-together, the weekend away, or the 12-hour football-watching holiday bash, and you may get some looks or sounds of major disapproval. Unless you come from a family of current or former graduate students, few will fully understand that which you are undertaking. So, there are really two huge challenges that face you (among dozens) when you are undertaking this dissertation: First, you are doing something immensely difficult that few people do. Second, your actions, because they are counter to the norm, don't easily fit with the world around you. It's as if the world is constructed for people to go to work, do just fine, make ends meet, and go home to have a meal and watch television. Anything more requires exceptional behavior.

Today, if your grand aspiration was to drive down the street and obtain a hamburger, I have no doubt that the skies would open up and assist you in every way to deliver that food unto your hands. If your desire was to binge-watch your favorite television show on demand for a few hours, I am sure that the time would present itself to make this happen. I also have little doubt that your family and your friends would bless you in these activities. However, abstain from a nearly-meaningless work-related meeting, be less available for the activities that are considered normal in your family or peer group, or act in any way like you are conserving time for the sake of a grand arrival that could be months or years down the line, and you will most definitely meet resistance. The world is not wired for your exceptional behavior — the behavior that is required to finish your dissertation and obtain the highest degree in the academic world. The world is seemingly wired for fast food, on-demand television, mediocre meetings, and left-behind goals. I say this because these are the things that come easy. Yet resolve to wake up earlier, get three hours to yourself for the sake of writing, or reserve 30 minutes of silence in the evening to do some reading, and the world does not rush to your aid. Instead, it can easily feel like the forces are stacked against you.

I recall going to Las Vegas when I was 21 years old and hitting the craps table. It's my favorite game, though gambling has become probably one of the least appealing activities in which I could engage — I hate losing. In the course of two hours, I turned $50 into $300. At the time, this was about 20 times my hourly wage. I left that table smiling…only to find myself frowning about 15 minutes later after mistakenly sitting at a shiny slot machine. I lost everything within a matter of minutes. Of course, there is a saying in Vegas, "The house always wins." It's as if the house is stacked against you from the moment you walk in. The odds are in the house's favor, after all! When it comes to the arduous task of writing hundreds of pages, poring through just as many sources, constructing a study, getting a team of people to agree with you on the contents of that study, and getting a university to give you the thumbs up to collect data for that study, the world at large is not accustomed to this being your focus. The house is stacked against you, in favor of entertainment, controversy, gossip, and crisis after crisis requiring your immediate attention. The odds are rigged to favor your *failure to finish this thing*. Are you going to let that happen?

To finish your dissertation, you must become accustomed to operating outside the norm and having people regard you as such. While many people in your life will flock to you in support of this amazing undertaking, few will understand fully what will be required of you. While your spouse, your children, your boss, and your coworkers may assist you in any way they can, unless they have gone through this process themselves, they don't fully understand what you are doing. When things get difficult and uncomfortable, return to the remembrance that there are oodles of people on this planet who want you to succeed — even if they lose sight of that from time to time. Without a doubt, there are those in your life who are fully willing to make the sacrifices required for you to finish this project. Still, there will be hard times. Just like the scene of sitting at a dinner table, politely passing the food to the next person when you are not partaking, there is a graciousness that is required of you to help them understand what you are doing. They require your support as much as you require theirs.

08

FOCUS ON THE 1%

Nearly every tale of enlightenment, every story about personal, professional, and spiritual transformation, focuses on a person who sees things differently. Another way of saying that is that the protagonists of most transformation tales simply were not paying attention to the same things as the vast majority of individuals around them. Jesus *could have* simply carried on his work as a carpenter's son, minding the mortgage and paying his taxes. Gautama Buddha could have stayed in his father's palace and enjoyed the splendors of courtly life instead of leaving royalty behind and becoming a starving ascetic living under a tree. The list goes on. I am constantly amazed by those who have the time, energy, and fortitude to ignore or transcend the, at times, insurmountable concerns of the day, including troubling supervisors, rising prices, stagnant wages, and the constant battle to find a sufficiently fast Wi-Fi connection. It truly takes a strong stomach and an impeccable mind to be able to not follow our instincts to look where everyone else is looking. As a high school teacher, I witnessed countless fights. The first clue of there being a fight was always a herd of 14- to 19-year-olds hurling their bodies the fastest they have moved in months, all to simply watch two human beings beat each other senseless, usually because one simply could not stop giving the other the Evil Eye. You have to ask yourself, "What causes human beings to all focus on the same things so consistently?" Frankly, we're pretty petty about that which commands our attention. If you wrote down all the things that get the time of your eyes, ears, mouth, nose, and mind, you might see that you are on a sensation binge on emotional and spiritual junk food, none of which is helpful in writing a dissertation.

With another political election behind us, I'm still flooded on social media with posts about what he or she did, what he or she is going to do, and what we should do about him or her in the coming months before he or she has a chance to do much worse. How is any of that information helpful for me to fulfill the purpose of my life, to make my spouse and my children more able to fulfill theirs, or to help the throngs of people I'm trying to help every day reach a lasting peace in their lives? How is anything on that television that is being sold to me by large companies that want me to buy stuff beneficial in helping me go in peace on my deathbed without regrets or remorse? It's like writing this book right now: I know that every word is going to make me more able to help you. I know that each word is going to help feed my family. I know that every single time that you share this book with someone else, my mission on this planet has come to fruition. I know without a doubt that someone will pick up this text a hundred years from now and gain something from it. Would I have better spent my time watching a rerun of a sitcom on my favorite streaming service? Would I have better spent my time complaining to another coworker about how someone treated me months or years ago? Would my time have been better spent being bored, browsing the web for something to buy to make me feel more complete for a few minutes? Would it have been better to simply give away my time to my email inbox and all those requests that are largely about other people's priorities instead of mine? My priority these days is becoming the best man I can be on this planet during my lifetime. My priority is doing well by my family and acting like every second of my time is a once-in-a-universe element that will one day run dry and I'll cease to be. The clock is ticking, and I don't have time to focus on stupid things. Frankly, you don't have time either — I know, not nice to say that, but you need to hear it. Time is ticking.

In so many parts of life, you could simply do the best by doing the complete opposite of most people around you. In the world of doctoral dissertations, there are many things that others will be doing while not finishing that will give you some clues about what you should focus on. Many of your peers at doctoral immersions, classes, and residencies will spend far more time dispensing advice about how to write a dissertation than actually writing one; I say focus on writing the darned thing without the advice of other novices. Many of your peers will be "writing" long before they have done enough reading, annotating, gathering, and outlining; I say spend more time reading in your fields of study, so that way, later on, you'll know what is worth writing. Many of your peers will be, understandably, crushed by the demands of life to the point where they have no time left to prioritize their dissertation work; I say what you give your first time to is your first priority — you have a choice to make about what is most important to you and second and so on. Just like those Olympians I was discussing earlier, who are on a strict diet, exercise regimen, and daily routine, one of the most profound ways you can make progress on your dissertation is by clearing your headspace of all the junk, trash, and excrement that gets airplay between your ears. The less noise there, the far more clarity you will experience in your day-to-day life under the demands of writing a doctoral study. It's like being in a small room with blaring rock music, all the while trying to listen consciously to your breath. You could fight the music, strain your mind and your attention to focus in and hear that open sound of your body reaching for air, or you could simply unplug the stereo and put it in storage for a day when you have more time to listen to that sort of stuff. Ninety-nine percent of what attempts to hijack your time is not worth it — not if time is of a limited quantity and you are writing a few hundred pages of text this year.

09

YOU ARE PART OF A FAMILY

No grand transformation occurs without some loss. The transformation into adulthood comes at the cost of losing childhood. The transformation toward married life comes at the loss of singlehood. The transformation toward health comes at the loss of old habits, old coping mechanisms, and old ways of interacting with the world. I state all this to point out that the transformation into doctoral life comes at a cost too: It comes at the cost of your time, your energy, your availability, and at times, your sanity. However, these losses are not simply experienced by you; they are experienced by everyone connected to you. I was recently speaking to a doctoral student during a one-to-one coaching session about her boss, who was now planning on firing her because she was no longer available 18 hours a day to be constantly at the beck and call of her supervisor. I recall a conversation a few months ago with a doctoral student whose adult children were increasingly frustrated that he was less able to come over on Saturdays or repeatedly answer texts during the week because he was spending so much time on his doctoral work. Even if you had the most disciplined doctoral life that fit perfectly within your schedule, others would still feel the loss of you no longer operating in the same ways in which you have been operating for years. You are part of a family, a community around you, that is "in this" just as much as you are — even though they aren't reading thousands of pages of text and spending just as many hours behind the keyboard. Just as I am writing this book to inform you about the ways in which you can come to your own support during this arduous writing process, I could easily write an entire other book about the way that this journey is going to impact others around you and how you could ease their pain.

You have to ask yourself, "What type of family member am I going to be during this process?" Assuming that you, indeed, are going to finish this thing, you have a few choices in front of you. First, you could be the *steamroller*, a family member who knows the direction he or she wants to head and simply continues forward without any regard for others or the consequences of his or her actions. You could schedule that writing time on a significant family or religious holiday, ignore tradition altogether, and simply "go rogue," absent, and unreachable. If you need that time on the weekend to write, you assume that your spouse will pick up the slack with the kids and that others will come to your aid — even though you have not asked them for such help. In this state, you know that with enough momentum, you will keep going in this project and make mammoth progress, crushing any obstacle in your path, regardless of the damage. "Darn it," you might say, "I deserve to get this thing done!" Is this the type of family member you want to be?

Alternatively, you could be the *passive passivist*, bending to the will of anyone or anything around you that you deem important. You have that standing Saturday writing time to get this dissertation done, but if someone needs you, you jump to that person's aid, cancel that writing, and simply say to yourself, "I'll make time later in the week to get this done." In this state, others rely on you for big things in your life. You have to be available for them, and they take a huge priority! This is, after all, your act of service in the world: to be the type of family or community member who is able to give your time, energy, and self for the cause of whatever. Not much writing gets done; though you do want to make progress, you are slammed by the forces around you. If you truly checked in with your family, you'd realize that they want big things for you too: They want you to finish! However, as things stand, progress is very slow because there simply is not enough of you to go around. Is this you?

Finally, you could take up the way of the *alchemist*: one who employs the forces all around him or her to the benefit of the ultimate good work that he or she is doing. You, after all, have a destiny beyond graduation that is calling to you. This dissertation work is not simply about getting another chit on your résumé. You are being called to big things! Accordingly, you speak with your family and community about what you are doing. You keep them informed about the sacrifices that they may need to make for the greater good that you are serving through your writing. In fact, you, personally, are willing to make huge sacrifices in your own life to get this work done. You are willing to work less. You are willing to spend less time watching television or playing with your phone. You are willing to prioritize your tasks at your job to accomplish those that are most critical because you know that you can't get everything done while you are working on this thing. You get to do this because others are fully aware of the magic that you are weaving in your life as a whole. You are doing something truly miraculous: You are trying to write hundreds of pages of text within only a handful of months. You are like those people whom they hear about: Those who climb mountains; those who lose oodles of unhealthy body fat; and those who write books, compose music, or create great works of art. You can be fully connected with everyone around you during this transformation — even as these individuals feel the loss of you during this process. Even during the hard times, you can be intimately present with members of your family, community, and peers who recognize that you are changing and that parts of the old you, ones that they very much enjoy, are less able to be present as you write one of the major works of your life.

DISSERTATION TIME TRAVEL

In this section, I describe how to accelerate your dissertation writing.

Additionally, I'll teach you how to be a more meaningfully productive being.

10

GET A GUIDE

Let's say a good friend of yours came into $50,000 in cash today and informed you that he or she would be investing that money into the stock market. Mind you, this friend knows nothing about the stock market, has never made money in there before, and has little or no training in stock market investing. This person tells you that he or she will have the chance to speak with a stock broker every few weeks or so for advice but will largely be doing this investing on his or her own. This individual enrolled in a few stock market investing courses offered by his or her broker. This friend has big dreams about what could happen! Thinking about this situation, what do you believe to be the likelihood of a positive outcome for this friend? What would have to happen in this situation to make it more probable for this investor friend to make some serious dough?

Similarly, let's say another friend of yours comes to you and tells you that he is planning on becoming a professional cage fighter. He's thrown a couple punches before in some beginning to intermediate martial arts classes and has even purchased a few books about how to become a cage fighter. His plan is to go to the gym every day each week for about 30 minutes. The gym he attends offers some free assistance from coaches who work there. The coaches can offer occasional advice and guidance and have helped a few other people become cage fighters. Considering this plan that your friend presents you, do you believe that this friend will succeed in his dream to be a successful mixed martial arts fighter? What would have to happen for this friend to succeed in this endeavor?

A paradox of academic life is that many look down on obtaining paid coaching — even though you are already paying dearly for your degree. You would pay someone to examine your car, assess your physical health, or even probe your emotions through therapy, but when it comes to obtaining paid writing tutoring, writing coaching, or editorial services (see note below), many treat such investments with a high degree of skepticism. You would pay tens of thousands of dollars for a car and pay hundreds to have such a car serviced. You would pay for a gym membership even if you did not meet your personal fitness goals. However, the idea of paying someone for academic coaching somehow strikes people as taboo. I admit that as a coach, I am biased. I believe that the videos, coaching, and tutoring I provide are of immense value to those I serve. When I sit on the phone with a client for one, two, or three hours, working through some of the logical problems in his or her drafts, I am often providing a service that the client can't obtain from his or her chair (though *some* are lucky to have chairs who *can* provide such attention and expertise). Further, if I can help one of my clients save three months of writing time, this could mean avoiding thousands of dollars' worth of paid continuation units — or the difference between graduating this year or next year — or missing the critical timing window in which to collect his or her data. In the end, I hope that doctoral students would consider, "How could paid assistance from a qualified tutor allow me to gain clarity and potentially save money and time?"

When considering utilizing paid services, here are some recommendations that I would like to offer:

1. Only utilize those services that are provided by real human beings who have a name and a face. Untrustworthy, faceless, so-called "dissertation farms" online do not deserve your hard-earned money or your time; they will ruin you.

2. You should know exactly what you are getting for what price. Many consultants will provide you with an hourly rate, package of coaching hours, or online videos, classes, etc. Ambiguous offerings should not be trusted. Ask clarifying questions.

3. If they offer to do any writing for you besides basic editorial services for spelling, grammar, and formatting, run for the hills. Utilizing providers who write anything for you is hugely dishonest and will likely result in your expulsion.

4. Differentiate between training, coaching, editing, and writing services. I solely provide training and coaching services. Training services include publications, online classes, books, etc. that describe how you can meet your dissertation goals. Coaching can take many forms but often deals with results (what you want to get done and how) and process (what challenges are arising in your process of writing). Editing services may or may not be allowed by your university. You should check. Editing services typically include help with spelling, grammar, and formatting. Writing services, usually banned by universities, and rightly so, often include fully constructed drafts of dissertations that are, nearly in all cases, a complete joke. Utilizing paid writing services where another human being is writing your paper for you is the height of laziness, dishonesty, and idiocy; anyone who does this deserves expulsion and public shaming.

5. Always ask, "Can I obtain what I am seeking for free at my university?" Chances are, you can! Many doctoral students will never utilize paid services during the writing of their dissertation. However, you may decide that you need the support, motivation, and/or expertise of a paid coach. Choose your mentor wisely.

11

FIVE BOOKS YOU NEED

There are five books that every dissertation writer should read besides this one. However, before I tell you the names of those books, I want to emphasize the difference between owning a book, consulting a text, and reading it. You probably have purchased many books you have never read. I'm not going to spend any time here guilting you about that; I have a personal library full of books that I have not yet had the chance to read. In the dissertation process, there are two primary ways that you will interact with a text. First, most often, you will read a portion of a text for the purposes of your literature search, literature review, and literary connections for your draft as a whole. During this reading, you could be said to be "consulting" this text. This means that you are not required nor do you need to read every word from cover to cover. Second, there are times when you will need to read a text — all of it, every chapter. There are VERY FEW such texts like this during your dissertation path. The following books are ones that you, indeed, will need to read fully, without missing much at all. Why? Because these texts are about the PROCESS of finishing. They are about the process of writing your dissertation. They are about the process of carrying out your methodology. They are about the process of analyzing your data. They are MANUALS that you will need to consult. Each should be read at a specific time of your writing process. However, you could obtain each text now, if you so wish. Also, as you purchase these texts, keep in mind that they are texts that you will return to time and time again after reading them. Accordingly, you may wish to purchase the texts in a format that matches your preference for such reference behavior (hard copy or eBook). Personally, I prefer hard copy for reference materials.

In order of purchase, here are the books you should obtain and read. For each, I describe the book's merits along with a suggestion of when the book may become part of your dissertation process:

1. The Journey-Map Text: ***The Dissertation Journey: A Practical and Comprehensive Guide to Planning, Writing, and Defending Your Dissertation*** (ISBN 978-1412977982), by Carol M. Roberts (2010), is the best guide that I have ever come across that describes the dissertation, explores each of its individual sections, and maps the "journey" from start to finish. This book is as much of an invaluable step-by-step guide as it is a map of the entire dissertation writing process from concept to defense and beyond. This book should immediately become part of your process. As you read it, I suggest starting from the first page and reading to the point of the writing process in which you currently sit. Most people reading the text I am typing on this page are writing their literature review. I suggest reading up until that point of Roberts's book until you are ready to move forward.

2. The Level One Methodology Text: The second book that you should obtain is one that helps you discover what methodology you *could* select for your study. Chances are, you have already decided whether you will be doing quantitative or qualitative work. Select the book that best matches your approach. If you are doing "mixed-methods" research, remember that mixed methods can often mean employing a combination of qualitative and quantitative processes, so you might need to get both books.

   a. Qualitative: ***Qualitative Inquiry and Research Design: Choosing Among Five Approaches*** (ISBN 978-1412916073), by John W. Creswell (2006), as the title describes, will help you differentiate between five potential qualitative methods. In particular, I have found this text helps doctoral students see the essential difference between case studies and phenomenological studies — a common error in methodology selection.

b. Quantitative: ***Educational Research: Planning, Conducting, and Evaluating Quantitative and Qualitative Research*** (ISBN 978-0133831535), by John W. Creswell (2014), describes many options for both qualitative and quantitative research. In terms of quantitative research, it will help you understand the basic options open to you (even though this has the word "educational" in the title).

3. The Deep-Cut Methodology Text: The third book that you should obtain after you have selected the methodology for your study will help you zoom in to best understand the exact procedural steps for the method you have chosen. Here are some of the best I've seen:

a. ***Quantitative and Statistical Research Methods: From Hypothesis to Results*** (ISBN 978-0470631829), by William E. Martin and Krista D. Bridgmon (2012)

b. ***Case Study Research: Design and Methods*** (ISBN 978-1452242569), by Robert K. Yin (2013)

c. ***Phenomenological Research Methods*** (ISBN 978-0803957992), by Clark Moustakas (1994)

d. ***Narrative Methods for the Human Sciences*** (ISBN 978-0761929987), by Catherine Kohler Riessman (2007)

e. ***Ethnography: Step-by-Step*** (ISBN 978-1412950459), by David M. Fetterman (2009)

f. ***Constructing Grounded Theory*** (ISBN 978-0857029140), by Kathy Charmaz (2014)

4. The Theoretical Framework Book: Next, you'll need to obtain a text for each main guiding theory that is at play in your study. In the social sciences, for example, I have seen many studies that invoke "integral theory," "critical race theory," and "transformational leadership theory." Often, theories such as these (at the time of writing this text, "grit" seems to be all the rage in educational research here in the United States) have seminal authors. Perform an internet search and see what major authors have created actual texts based on these theories or areas of study. Books such as these contribute to your understanding of the individual components of the theoretical framework or frameworks you've selected for your research.

5. The Style Manual: Finally, you'll need to obtain the handbook for the specific style that you are utilizing in your study. For example, if you are utilizing APA style for your work, you'll need to obtain that official publication manual. It can be tempting to rely solely on internet resources for your formatting questions because they are free. Conversely, some dissertation writers feel they can fully rely on their editors to fix the problems of their text later, forgetting that such editors often charge by the hour for their services. Most important, however, is being able to communicate in the style that your university has selected as part of the portfolio of scholarly skills you are soon going to embody.

In the end, remember that buying a text is far less important than reading the text, annotating it, and soaking in the soul of what it means to do the type of research you are aspiring to do. You are becoming a researcher; you are not just doing research. It's time to get these books and dive in, cover to cover.

12

GO INTO THE CLOSET

After my first child was born, I would often try to write and do other creative tasks inside my home. After all, I grew up with my dad working down the hall from my bedroom. For me, the idea of working inside my house has always held an allure of mystery, reminiscent of those days I would wake up as a five-year-old to the smell of menthol cigarettes trailing from down the hallway, the night silence peppered with the persistent clacking of my dad's fingers on ancient IBM keyboard keys. As a youngster, I would walk down the hallway before the sun was up and peer around the corner to see him sitting with his back to me, already in his polyester shirt and pants, leather loafers, gold chains, and slicked back hair. He was doing something revolutionary for the time: He was making a substantive living working from his own home office, working via a computer connection over the phone to cities throughout the world. "This is what being a man looks like," I would think. So, it was by no mistake that I set up my own home office and tried to emulate this behavior — minus the waking up at 3:00 a.m. part. I experienced a significantly lower level of success as a creator, writer, and entrepreneur in my arrangement because I was immediately available to the stresses of life. There was no barrier between me and the chaos. There was nothing romantic about working in my home, in a coffee shop, or in any other public place because I found myself too accessible. You might be experiencing the same stresses, thinking, "Where can I possibly go to get any of this work done without interruption?" When speaking with dissertation writers, I often tell the story of how I came to make significant progress on my own dissertation. It began with renting a closet.

During my first year out of doctoral coursework, I wasted much of my time making futile attempts at jumping into the dissertation project for a few days, only to fall out to the pressures of beating the next level of Legend of Zelda or pursuing my next big career move. I am a very distractible person. The big change for me came when I asked my father-in-law if I could utilize a vacant "work space" in his office — a 10-foot-by-10-foot space that was largely filled with filing cabinets and bad, dusty ventilation. I found that if I could be inside that office space by 7:00 a.m. each day, I could get loads of work done without any interruption at all — very few people knew I was there, and almost no one knew how to reach me. Often, this morning ritual would yield eight-hour days of dissertation work. I often alternated between working 45 minutes, walking around the parking lot for 15, and returning for another round of 45. These 45/15/45 spurts of effort in a space that was unknown to most human beings in my life allowed me to complete my literature review in only a couple months' time. After working for years on a single chapter of my dissertation, I found myself writing two of them within 10 weeks. Everything I had experienced as a doctoral researcher up until that point provided me with the skill to be able to do this — but it was the space, hidden away from so many others, that allowed me to have the time to get the writing done.

You should strongly consider securing a hidden workspace somewhere. Considering the cost of paying continuation units to your university for the pleasure of NOT completing your dissertation, the minute expense of a ratty office space (some of which I have seen in California for only $150 a month with internet) could be well worth your time. Imagine having a place where you could set up your stacks of books, your computer, your mounds of paper, and your favorite snack food items and beverages, all so you can work, hidden away in peace. What if you had a place that you and your family could agree was yours only and that when you were there, no interruptions would be tolerated? It's not that you'd ignore problems that would arise in your friendships and family while in this space, but you would carefully and creatively decide when the phone was going to be disconnected or off so that you could work uninterrupted.

Similarly, consider the power of only checking your email at carefully chosen times during the day so that you don't fall victim to someone hijacking your schedule because of a "crisis" that the person could have warned you about weeks ago. As for me, I check email at 10:00 a.m. and 2:00 p.m. During my dissertation writing, I had an automated outgoing email message that would inform people of this schedule, providing my phone number for "emergencies," which had a carefully crafted definition. I would stay off social media during writing times. I modified my device settings to prevent notifications from arising during this time. During even crazier writing times, I used a specialized piece of security software to disable my internet for an hour without the possibility of re-enabling it. I would only give myself permission to eat after a paragraph was completed. I would leave the office only if I had met my daily minimums: five sources read, five quotes from each source recorded, five sources filed away. I conspired with my wife to provide smaller rewards for smaller benchmarks being met in my writing. I did all this from the security and far-away, removed safety of my holy workspace that was only for this grand work of getting this dissertation done. When my body entered this space, its only purpose was to become the man who was ready to come into being after graduation. Create the space for great work to be done, get your body in there, and great work will often emerge as a result. All you have to do is get there and stay there until something happens. Will you show up?

———————————————————

13

WHAT GETS TIME FIRST?

One of my colleagues — a young man in what would probably be, under normal circumstances, the middle of his life — died a few weeks ago. I laid in bed last night in the dark and thought of the horror of it all: his wife, his kids, his friends, the course of the past couple years that led to this. Truly, "running out of time" is my greatest fear: running out of time to do the good that I seek to do in the world — for my wife, for my kids, for me. It's become a daily contemplation: What if today is all I have? What then? For me, this is not a hopeless mindset. There's a chance for living well, living more healthfully, living in the reality of things: I only have so much time to do what I can in the world. Doing my work with such a thought in my heart changes everything.

I've been thinking a lot about my kids too. They only get so much of me, after all. How much of them do I put off because someone is hounding me via email for something that is not really that important or truly could have been taken care of weeks ago if planning was executed more effectively? How much of their youth and my influence in their life am I putting aside because I am flicking through my Facebook® feed or reading about *whatever* happening in the world today? I am coming to see myself more and more like a self-sourced jam band artist who has some major contributions to bring to those whom I am communing with on a daily basis. Am I robbing them by taking part in the daily junk-food buffet with which the world of convenience wants to fill my heart and mind? I would be ashamed of myself if I drank myself into a stupor and was unable to be there fully for my children the next day because of my indulgence. Why would I not feel the same way about all the nonsense on which I spend my time? What if the greatest parts of me that I have a chance to impart to the world — including my kids, my wife, and all those around me I call my community — were wasted all because I could not buck up and let go of the needless distractions of busyness?

A transformation has been occurring in me, and I challenge you to follow me in starting your day in service of higher aspirations. Rather than slogging out of bed and stumbling into a cup of coffee and straight into emails, I ask you to consider what deserves your freshest energy: That deserves your time most. Make a list of everyone with whom and everything with which you will come into contact during the course of a day. Rank these forces from most important, deserving your best energy, to least important, perhaps not warranting any energy or attention whatsoever. Tragically, when you do this, as I daily do, you may find that you have been ransoming your most precious hours, heart-space, and brainpower to tasks that don't rank high on the list. Worst yet, you may regularly see that it's the tasks that rank on the middle to lower end of the list that pay the bills. As of the writing of this, I am not yet brave enough to suggest that you throw out every item that ranks low on the list in service of those that rank higher. However, I do challenge you to give the top three or four items your best time. Do they not, at least, deserve an hour or so? Thirty minutes? Ten minutes?

Yesterday, I was working with a doctoral candidate who has been "all but dissertation" (ABD) for over two years. Suddenly, within the span of three weeks, she finished both her literature review and her methodology chapters (over 70 pages of writing completed). In her experience, this happened because of three coalescing forces. First, she realized that she had "banked" a considerable amount of sick and vacation time with her employer. Second, she and a friend, over a glass of wine, realized that she would be *less able* to take time off in the future unless she finished this doctoral degree. Third, she had done enough prewriting. Finally, she decided to take a "dissertation vacation," where she sat on the shore of a lake in New England for 21 days with only aspirations to eat, drink, and write. With these singular aims, she successfully gained some weight and furthered her word count. Without fail, she wrote from 8:00 a.m. until 4:30 p.m., reserving the final 30 minutes of her post-writing workday for answering emails, calling her office, and working with those problems to which she would typically dedicate 90% of her time during the business day. Because she was servicing her top three priorities (health, happiness, and finishing her doctoral studies), results followed.

As I write this to you, I know that I am servicing my highest calling in life to be a servant of God. If today I have stirred in you any sense of discomfort, excitement, or even permission, I have lived in service of that highest heart within you that is wanting you to finish this thing. Even if you don't believe in all of that, it does not take away from this investment of my time that I am making on behalf of you, my children, my spouse, and me. Think about it: When your time is well spent on a task that feeds the highest callings of your heart and mind, how can anyone take that accomplishment away from you? As you invested your time to read my words here, you served your calling to finish. No one, nothing, can take away the blessing that you gave to yourself by spending just five minutes on your dissertation by reading this text, browsing through an online database, or clicking the keys for a short while inside your draft. Even further, imagine living your whole life this way: only giving time to those things that truly mattered. What if more people around you did that too? What would that world look like? Today, I challenge you to give 10 minutes to something that matters to you — dissertation or not. Then, post a picture of that on my Facebook® page.

www.facebook.com/TheDissertationMentor

14

YOU DON'T NEED TO BE FANCY

It's easier to buy things related to writing your dissertation than to actually write it. In our online community, I've seen people buy desks, chairs, cars, pens, software, vacation packages, timeshares, computers, shelving, wood flooring, pets, religious icons, bottled water and juice subscriptions, cookies, phones, editing services, statistical services, and, yes, even books, instead of writing their dissertation. One candidate even bought a library of books (hundreds of texts) before he opened a single page and began reading. Beyond the potential lack of need for some of these items, the sheer cost of some of these purchases would bring anyone to a pause. Do you really need a $300 pen to feel like you are doing important work? In a materialist culture, "buying" behaviors have been engrained into us as "productive" behaviors. Even worse is that some, at some level, equate the purchases they make with a sense of identity. They think, "Having this brand-new computer with the latest and most expensive statistical analysis software makes me a dissertation writer!" Little could be further from the truth; the only thing that makes you a dissertation writer is that you are writing your dissertation. No purchase can supplant your eyes gliding across a page or your fingers hammering on the keyboard of your choice.

Dissertation writing is, at its best, scrappy, dirty, sweat-worthy work that does not need to be conducted with a golden pen and embossed leather-covered books inside one's lakeside, rented vacation home whilst listening to music on the latest, greatest music player over the world's most price-accessible high-end speakers from a $300 office chair. You'll probably get more done at the local Wi-Fi-ready pub or (my favorite) inside a dank $200-a-month closet rented from one of the local businesses down the street. You don't need to be fancy to get great work done. In fact, it's the attempt at being fancy, wanting everything to be perfectly in its place and of the highest quality, that robs one of the ability to get great work done. Ask anyone who has completed a dissertation, and that person will probably tell you that some of the best work came from the least ideal circumstances: When the only things available to that individual were time, a writing instrument, and a book, progress materialized.

Dissertation writers often become obsessed with ideal circumstances. They say to themselves, "I need to write for at least an hour — and now that I don't have an hour, I can't write at all."

Or, "My internet connection is wonky, so I can't do anything about this dissertation today."

Or sometimes, "My chair has not returned his feedback to me, so there simply is no way that I can do anything about this project until he returns my email."

Or worse, "This is not the right season of life for me to be working on this right now; a better time will come."

Sadly, it's through this mindset of "I need things to be just right" that they lose the chance to leave all excuses behind and get great work done. After all, self-talk like those sentences listed above is a great hint that you are almost out of excuses for getting any work done. When the mental stop sign appears saying, "You better not work on this right now" or "You can't do this until this other thing happens" or "You need to buy this other thing to be able to read/write," you can take solace in knowing that your brain is completely full of it and that it's time to sit down and start working. In fact, a strategy you should employ — one that I recommend to nearly every dissertation writer with whom I come into contact — is to immediately give your dissertation no less than 15 minutes of work, without hesitation, should your brain come up with any excuse not to read or write. In terms of your dissertation work, it's always better to work on it now, as the more time you wait, the more stale the project will become, and a cycle of "not doing, feeling down, so not progressing" will ensue, and it will haunt you until you finish — or until you give up, only to have it haunt you later in life that you did not finish. Hesitation is the signal that it's the perfect time to start reading or writing.

In our cultures, we often respect the underdog — and I hope that you will pick up the mantle of being the scrappy, dirty, sweating underdog. In no film ever did we respect and admire the great rich dude who had it all figured out while he got richer without challenges and then lived happily ever after before dying; I never saw anything like this in theaters because it's boring. The life that sounds more interesting to me is the one that begins with an everyday life, one that you were called from into doctoral studies, and now you are facing the dragon of this dissertation, and you have two options: Use the tools at hand to defeat it or go back home from whence you came. Truly, I hope you will pick up your cheap, corner-market pen and start writing. I hope that you will get yourself to any local university library and start poring through its stacks. I hope that every single excuse for not working will be extinguished — because time is running out, and you deserve to finish. It's in your best interest to finish. The road ahead is not easy, and not much will make it easier beyond doing the work. So put this book down and get to work.

15

YOU HAVE TIME TO WRITE THIS DISSERTATION

Dissertation writing is not an "average man's" endeavor. The average person's consumption of video, email, social media, food and drink, and concern/outrage/worry over trivial matters leads to a false sense of security based on busyness of body and mind. Sadly, most people don't realize that this brand of busy is actually one of the most prevalent forms of laziness on the planet. Most people don't spend their day lounging; the vast majority of breathing humans today will spend their day rushing from one task to another, often feeling as if they don't have time for it all. "Working hard" is not rare in this world. To break away from the average and do something as monumental as finishing one's dissertation requires renunciation: The formal, intentional rejection of behaviors that you know will not contribute to your long-term happiness. Renunciation is like bravely choosing not to have cookies for every meal because while they may taste good in the moment, the result of a short-lived life of multi-meal cookie consumption cannot and will not lead to long-term satisfaction or happiness.

To finish this dissertation, you'll have to renounce many sacred practices that are held dear by you, your family, your coworkers, and the culture at large around you. At one of my more recent places of employment, the generally accepted practice was that email was to be checked multiple times an hour and immediately addressed. Throngs of educators were keeping their email clients active on their computers and running to delete or reply every time that "bong" was heard over their speakers. If you went a few hours without responding, the feeling was that you, somehow, were not doing your job. Should you take more than 10 hours to respond to a student's email request, you were considered entirely "non-responsive." Accordingly, the culture of online engagement was always as shallow as the importance of the fire being hurled from someone else's office into one's inbox. Often, I thought disconcertingly, "Why is the lack of planning on the part of this person my immediate responsibility to manage?" "How can I do my great work if I am always helping others do theirs?" "When do WE get to do great work together because we are not spending all our time on smaller concerns?" In the case of this workplace, I left before I was outed as a complete heretic. It's proven to be one of the best moves of my life.

What are some of the sacred, habitual practices in which you, your family, and your coworkers engage that need to be left behind? We often fall into what's workable for us. We fall into a routine that makes sense given the circumstances of the work we do, the hours we have available, and the energies that we have at our disposal at any given part of the day. It's one of the most challenging endeavors during the dissertation process, and in the rest of life, to make the conscious choice to renounce and leave aside that which makes us the most comfortable and secure to do the great work that we feel called to complete — the work that goes beyond just paying the bills and going home to relax for a brief period each night. The world would be satisfied if you went to work every day, stayed safe, paid your bills, and made small, incremental gains in the quality of your lifestyle each year until you retired and then expired. To do something more may require extreme measures, like turning off your phone for an hour each day, only accessing Facebook® after 7:00 p.m. each evening, checking your email at four preset times throughout the day, or choosing to listen to more uplifting, nourishing media. It's like being an older child and becoming a young adult by deciding to put down the toys in favor of other activities. You've done it before, and you can do it again. You'll have to.

More than hard work, renunciation requires discipline. Where hard work typically connotes long hours, an overload of tasks to complete, and probably stress, discipline is exertion with a strong focus alongside loads of renunciation. Discipline in dissertation writing means getting up every day before the sun to do 60 minutes of reading or writing. Discipline is working on this paper every single day for a month without fail. Discipline is purposefully avoiding foods and beverages that make you tired so that you'll have more energy stored later on. Discipline is shutting down all screens for an hour before going to sleep so that you can be more rested and ready for the next day's work. Discipline is something that the brain loves because there is a great deal of habit involved. Once the habit takes root — some say it takes 21 days — it begins to perpetuate itself. The fruit of this brand of discipline over enough time will produce a finished paper to hand your chair or principal advisor.

You have time to write this dissertation because you have the time to do plenty of other things. You can be like the woman who took 15 extra minutes before lunch to find a quiet room and meditate in silence each day and, because she consistently employed this practice, found she was significantly more productive and present with her work later in the afternoon. You can be like the man who turned his phone off for the first two hours after returning home; he spent the first hour working on his dissertation and the other simply being available to talk with his teenage children. You can be like me, giving up another episode of some old show on some streaming service simply so I could type this line of text this evening. No matter the state of your schedule, there is a chance to put something down and pick up your dissertation.

16

SLEEP LESS

At 4:30am, the coffee tastes better, the internet is faster, and every human being who seeks to disrupt my work is unconscious. At 5am, I get more done than any other part of the day, my brain is focused (because it's not awake enough to worry), and I have the added benefit of feeling impressed with myself for getting up before the vast majority of human beings in my country. By 6am, when most people are waking up, I've already finished the most important project of the day — my writing — just in time for my children to begin to stir, for the TV to pop on for morning cartoons, and for my bride to start emerging from the blanket of sleep. Before anyone even notices, the project of the highest priority is addressed. Far before "the system," which seeks to keep us compliant, earning, and purchasing, even is aware, I've already beat it. By 6:30am, when I'm showered and ready to run off to work, I've already won the day — and it's only just begun. The day is better as a result. The evenings are reflective times of peace — more so than ever before — all because I chose to wake early rather than letting my children decide what time they will wake me up or giving my boss the satisfaction of knowing that he required me to have my car entering the parking lot by a certain time of day. By deciding for myself to wake early, I prize my time, and that which fills it, more than anything else on this planet.

Chances are, in your dissertation work, you are attempting to make this mammoth project fit within the confines of an already overly busy life. I have the impression, based on my many conversations with candidates from over 50 countries, that you may be scheduling your dissertation work either (a) after work time or (b) on your boss's time. In the first scenario, work hours are finished, and you stay at work late, retreat to some local coffee shop, or come home and start your dissertation work. Often, at this time, you are the most exhausted and least resilient. Your brain is foggy, tired, and is constantly asking you to stop working, have dinner, turn on the television, have a glass of wine (or tea), and head to bed while playing with your phone. Additionally, you have your loved ones, who care for you greatly and want your attention, to contend with. If you opt to steal your boss's time to get this project done, you feel anxious, keeping your screen away from the view of passersby, unable to have dissertation-related books strewn about your desk. God forbid that you attempt to print something — having to run to the queue before anyone notices that you, a mid-level manager, are printing uncharacteristically scholarly journals on the networked copy machine. Either way, your brain and your heart are working against you: Few want to steal time away from their place of employment or their family or their personal rest time to write a multi-hundred-page doctoral paper. Why, then, torture yourself with these two horrible options?

Two years ago, I was fortunate enough to be blessed by my bride to be able to attend a week-long meditation retreat in Eagle Rock, California. The typical day began just around sunrise, and each day would end at sunset, including long periods of sitting meditation interspersed with walking meditation and teachings. On the first day, the excitement of being part of such an activity was joyously overwhelming — driving there before the sun came up, being there for the opening convocation, sitting for those initial hours, and knowing that I was doing something good for myself and my family. By the third day, it was very challenging knowing that this routine would produce an opening for something new but knowing that it would take great effort to sustain for the remainder of the week. By day six, waking up early for a whole day of "work" was effortless, joyful, and something that I had learned to appreciate. For me, this experience emulates what you might feel in the course of waking up early on the first day of your "new season" of concentrated work on your dissertation. You'll be somewhat excited, lost, unsure of what to expect, and very hopeful. By the third day, waking up could be a significant challenge. However, by the time you get to the end of the week, choosing to continue this practice into the next, you'll feel as if this was something that you should have done months ago.

Still, you must guard your sleep. As I mentioned in the previous chapters, the quality of our activities during the day have a significant impact on our sleep. The food and media we consume and the social activities in which we take part change the way that our brains can rest during the night time. The chemicals that are released in the brain during times of great stress and trauma can, very much, be flowing during the course of our normal day's work. What we have come to accept as normal daily activity is actually killing us. I always tend to tilt my head to one side in confusion whenever I hear someone talking about watching post-apocalyptic dramas on television — as if the world in which we live was not traumatic enough! Similarly, just as being around someone who's constantly spewing negative, salacious gossip can be draining, being embedded within an organization that is untrustworthy, like a 9:00 a.m. to 5:00 p.m. North Korea, could be damaging your quality of rest as well. My personal conviction is that we do live, in part, to do work, but we can do GREAT WORK above all else. Through the discipline of getting great rest and then waking up to an intentionally productive day, you can get more done in the coming weeks than you ever have in the breadth of your doctoral work thus far. Do you dare set your alarm and not allow it to snooze?

17

ONE MINUTE TURNS INTO 10 MINUTES

Parkinson's law states that a task will expand to fill the time allotted to it. If you give a scheduled meeting an hour's time, the meeting will probably last an hour (or longer). Give yourself three hours to relax, and I imagine your rest will fill at least that time. Conversely, in the absence of time-space for the task to take place, it most likely will not happen. Why, then, do so many dissertation writers expect to finish their dissertation even when no time has been provided for them to write it? For many candidates, it's not that they are not willing to provide the time required; it's that they think in too large a scale of work to be able to go to task, get reading, start typing, and get any meaningful scholarly work completed. Rather than thinking in 10-minute units of time, they are thinking in larger, three-hour blocks of time. While three-hour blocks are most definitely the ideal, these individuals rarely find they have such swaths of time available. Nothing happens. No writing occurs. For years, they don't have much happening in their writing life. Accordingly, they grow depressed, angry, or anxious about the process as a whole; as a result, even less work happens. Today, I am directly making a request of you: I am asking you to give yourself some time each day. Give your dissertation 10 minutes, without fail, six days per week.

In my own writing practice, the 10-minute rule is absolute. I can't call myself a writer if I am not writing. It's a lot like being a dad and a husband: There are certain ways of being with and around my family that must happen, or I am not a husband or a father. For me, keeping the standard high, holding myself to certain set-points of success each day provides an immensely needed sense of grounding. I know that you have often felt lost in this dissertation writing process. You ask yourself, "Am I making progress? Am I going to finish? When am I going to finish?" You say to yourself, "I'm not making progress. I'm going round and round in circles. I'm rewriting this section for the third time!" In absence of knowing if you are progressing, you are left with the chance of going a bit crazy, like a desert wanderer who has been marching toward a mirage for days in search of shade and water, never knowing if he or she is getting any closer than the day before. Always, the goal feels like it's far on the horizon. So, when you put a line in the sand yourself, saying, "I will give this 10 minutes today," you have the mark of success by which to gauge yourself. It's a manageable mark. It's doable. Everyone has 10 minutes somewhere in his or her schedule. You too can be a dissertation writing badass today just by sitting down and giving yourself some time to work on this thing. Give your dissertation 10 minutes.

Admittedly, I'm running a bit of a scam by asking you to give 10 minutes because I know that if you truly give 10 uninterrupted minutes to your dissertation, you will probably give 15 or 30 or 60 minutes to your dissertation once you have the courage to close the door, turn off the phone, shut down the email, and start reading or writing. Like being at the gym, now that you are here exercising and all other potential distractions are locked outside, taking a few more minutes to do another set of reps or play with another exercise machine is not a big deal. Repeated over the span of six days, the result could be an hour working on your dissertation or more, all because you gave some time each of those days without fail. If you have the appropriate office or desk at work, I recommend going there about 30 minutes earlier than usual and using that for your dissertation work. Alternatively, buy a coffee pot with a timer and hide it in your secret, rented office space and get into the car and get over there first thing in the morning. When you give 10 minutes to a task like this, progress begins to appear because the opening was present so that the work could get done.

Writing this book that is in your hands or on your screen right now was not some miracle occurrence: If you looked at my calendar each day, you'd see that the impossible is made possible through a little sliver of time etched out in the early morning hours before I check my email, meet with my bosses and colleagues, or even drink my second cup of coffee. Ten minutes every day, which typically becomes about 30 to 45 minutes, becomes dozens of hours over months. It allows a small outline in my word processor to start becoming (at this moment) a 208-page, double-spaced document. Like the artist who slowly chipped away at a block of marble to make an iconic statue during the Renaissance, the hardest work is NOT finishing the statue; the hardest work is getting up every day, putting the chisel and hammer in your hands, and getting busy on that heavy rock. Once you repeat that enough days, the final product will start materializing through your hard work. The point is to pick up the tools, get into your workshop, and set a timer for 10 minutes.

18

CHUNK IT

When you put a bunch of rabbits in a pen together, they create more rabbits. Our brains work in a similar fashion. Repeat a task for a number of minutes and you ease into a flow of work that is faster than when you started. Imagine sitting with a thousand envelopes needing to be stuffed. The first 30 or so stuffings would be the most time consuming; your brain and body would be learning how to fold the papers, how to best slip them into the envelopes, and how to seal the parcels. Meanwhile, your emotions would be playing the tricks of "Do we really want to be doing this?" or "Couldn't you hire this out to someone else?" or "Shouldn't we be working on our dissertation?" However, after the initial repetitions, you would begin to get into a state of flow that would allow you to complete more and more stuffings until you hit a plateau of potential, the fastest that you could humanly put papers into envelopes, slowing over time with the energy and stamina of your body. Your dissertation work can be quite similar. In the previous chapter, I talked about simply giving 10 minutes, which, naturally, could lead to more and more time being spent on the dissertation. Here, I want to point out that what often prevents you from getting much work done on your dissertation, among procrastination, stress, and generally feeling overwhelmed, is that you, frankly, could be making dissertation work too complicated. It's time to simplify.

At the start of the 20th century, Henry Ford's assembly line simplified the ridiculously expensive and time-consuming task of building an automobile. Ford did this by assigning each worker a specific, small (very small) set of tasks that would be repeated over and over again. Each person became an expert on his or her individual piece of car-work. What Ford found, and as we have observed since, is that when you put a specific task in front of a person (as opposed to the huge project as a whole), that person is often able to complete that task — and potentially repeat it again and again. Over a long enough time period, significant progress can manifest. For example, if your chair asked you to "Go and write your dissertation," this is a huge goal that is most worthy of your time but is often too huge in scale to work on in a single sitting. This would lead to a sense of feeling lost, overburdened, and helpless. Consider what would happen if that same chair asked you to "Go and find me five books about your topic, and send me those titles." Now, this task is exceedingly manageable. In fact, you KNOW you can do this task. So, you get online or go to the library, and you find these five books — success. This is possible because the scale of the task is sufficiently low that accomplishing it is not only possible, it's easy. Repeat this book-finding challenge 20 times, and you've found 100 books potentially worthy of appearing in your literature review. Do the same for journal articles and dissertations, and you have the full means to write most, if not all, of your introduction and literature review. Reduce the scale of the tasks in which you engage for your dissertation: Chunk it.

The average reader of this book is working through his or her literature review. To chunk down this task, you could do the following:

Monday: Find 10 full-text articles about a single subject relating to your dissertation. Download them and print them only.

Tuesday: Visually skim (do not read) these 10 full-text articles. In orange highlighter, mark the sections that you intuitively feel deserve to be read word-for-word.

Wednesday: For five of the articles, read those sections you marked the day before. Using a yellow highlighter, shade only those sections that *could* end up in your dissertation as direct quotations (note: they WON'T end up as direct quotations, but they could potentially).

Thursday: Repeat Wednesday's task for the other five articles.

Friday: For each of the 10 articles, write a short, one-sentence synopsis of the number one, main notable contribution that the article makes to your examination of the literature thus far.

Saturday: Transcribe all your notes into a document.

Sunday: Celebrate. Feel good about yourself. You are doing it!

Notice how the above list probably sounds more manageable than your dissertation may have felt in recent history. The above schedule assumes somewhere between 15-30 minutes of work each day. Easily, you could do more than this. You could turn 10 articles into 20. The key, regardless, is that you must keep each individual task separate. Never combine different tasks into the same session of work. Never switch from your internet browser displaying your online journal article to Facebook®. Don't attempt to download, read, and annotate the articles in the same sitting. In the least, do one task, take a short break, and then return and delve into the next task. Should you switch from one task to another, your brain will switch gears, slow you down, and lose that momentum that you've been building for the minutes prior. Your task is to keep the momentum going through concentrating on a single task for a set number of minutes, pages, citations, or quotations. Then, take a break. Repeat this for a few handfuls of weeks, and you'll have the makings of a literature review. Make the pledge to not drive yourself crazy — chunk tasks for progress.

19

GO DARK

I recently dreamt that the Dow dropped to 10.00, that there was a worldwide epidemic of alcoholic mothers, and that I needed to protect my son from some unseen evil force, all in the span of a dream that, I imagine, only lasted a few minutes right before my alarm woke me up at 5:00 a.m. A few minutes later, sitting wrapped in a blanket on my couch in the dark with my phone in one hand and a cup of coffee in the other, I was reading the news and seeing some familiar plot points emerging: "Stock market fears…"; "Substance abuse among women…"; "Local child abducted…." Later that day, writing one of the opening chapters to this book, I found myself distracted by some of the news stories that I had read before. In the back of my head, the dream had still shaken me, the news had still created anxiety in me, and I found my mind wandering to subjects that, while important in some respects, really had no practical use for me for the task at hand: finishing this book. This illustrates a concept that I teach every doctoral learner: Like a future Olympian in training, you need to avoid junk food, junk drink, junk sleep, and above all, junk thinking, especially that brought on by junky people and junky media. Avoid these, lest they impact your work, your family, and your happiness. When you walk into your hidden dissertation lair to get your reading and writing done for the day, the forces of darkness — or the forces of junk — will attempt to follow you. They will sit on your shoulder and distract you. They will lie to you because change is dangerous to them. They would rather you sit with a bag of potato chips on your couch watching another episode of whatever. They would rather you grow old in regret for not finishing this thing. It's time to shut them out — to cut them off.

It's not just you that enters that room. In with you come preoccupations with bills, grades, calls, emails, bosses, spouses, ex-lovers, regrets, suffering, junk food, gossip, junk news, and a whole host of other concerns that have ZERO practical use when writing your dissertation. Everything that is in your life will have an impact on what you do within that room in your reading, annotating, transcribing, outlining, and studying. Accordingly, you have to address what is happening outside the room. Outside your den of dissertation greatness, be mindful of what you are consuming in food, drink, media, and sleep. Hold some caution about getting too easily sucked into the drama of those around you, the inflated catastrophes in the news, or the persistent, unsubstantiated fears related to bosses, work, and academia. As a dear friend and teacher said to me, "You can't *dabble* in sanity; it's a full-time gig." Accordingly, I encourage you to make a practice of guarding your mind and holding everything that seems so serious and grave with a sense of levity — as if that which 99% of people think is true probably is not as true as they think. After all, the stock market correcting or crashing has zero impact on my ability to write today. Your boss's feelings about your performance, completely not grounded in reality, will not make any difference in the project of finishing this text. The "emergencies" that take up so much time in people's lives, and, accordingly, take up so much of our own lives, are not of our creation — we've done our jobs and deserve to have the time to accomplish whatever we set our hearts toward. So, outside your writing cave, you must guard against the intrusions of neurotic fears and habitual indulgences in the drama of the people in the world around you. Create a healthy mood of both humor and skepticism in all your dealings. Often, things are not as bad as they seem, and there is ALWAYS a chance for change — always.

Inside your protected, closed-off dissertation laboratory, you have to contend solely with yourself. You will be tempted to keep the phone on, to keep the email window open, to answer that text message, or to watch one more video unrelated to your dissertation. My suggestion is to leave the phone in the car, if you can. Utilize a tool like Freedom (https://freedom.to/) to temporarily disable your internet connection for a preset time. Assure your mind, while your egg timer is clicking next to you for your designated 10, 30, or 60 minutes, that everything that is outside your door will STILL BE THERE when you get done with this segment of reading or writing, so you don't need to address any of that right now. Say to yourself repeatedly, like a chant, "I have a right to my time on this planet." Go dark from the world, cut yourself off from everyone for a time, and get your checkboxes for the day slashed so that you can say to yourself before going to bed, "Today, I worked on my dissertation." You don't have to sacrifice your time, happiness, sense of accomplishment, or life to the forces that attempt to control you. You have just as much right, if not more, to finish this dissertation and fulfill your aspirations as your employer has for you to finish a project or respond to a silly email.

Today, I'm thinking of a dear woman in my life who has given everything to her kids and her husband. She sacrificed everything for them year after year. Her family is good for it. Yet my recent conversations with her children, who are old enough now to see the kind of person their mother is, revealed that they wish that she, now in her elderly years, had spent more time doing, accomplishing, and being the person SHE WISHED she could be throughout her life. Many of their sentences were framed like, "She could have missed just one game…"; "She could have spent one less hour…"; "She could have just taken one afternoon to…." As you are in your place of writing, remember that those who love you want you to finish. They want you to take the time you need to finish this dissertation.

20

FINAL DRAFT PLEDGE

When I was eight years old, my dad bequeathed to me the family lawnmower and said, "Go forth, my son," pointing at our one-acre parcel, "and cut grass." Thus, a 10-year near-weekly ritual of getting outside on a Saturday or Sunday to mow the lawn was born. It was a grueling affair for me as a young person. In our inland suburb of Los Angeles, the temperature would climb to around 105 degrees Fahrenheit (40 degrees Celsius) in the summertime. The process involved "weed-whacking" the edges, mowing the lawn, and hauling the refuse out to our collection bins. Typically, it was about a two-hour affair. My dad, who had mastered our huge yard with elaborate landscaping, decorative plants, fencing, trees, patios, and a pool, would often appear, dark framed behind the front or back screen door of our house, holding a semi-clear, blue plastic glass filled with iced tea or lemonade. He would take a slow, dramatic sip with one hand on his hip and grunt, "Eeeeeeee 'boy, you missed a spot over there." If there was any humor in his voice, it was not accepted by my adolescent brain. It became a torture to have him see my work in progress and ridicule my efforts when they were not even finished. Further, I noticed that the earlier in the process he observed, the more fault he would find with my work, and inevitably, this would cause more work later on. My solution: Get up at 6:30am, when he was still groggily stammering out of bed, fumbling for a cup of coffee, and flipping on CNN on the television, and start mowing the lawn. By the time the caffeine had taken the intended effect in his bloodstream and he had sufficiently learned what was happening in the OJ Trial, in the Bush

1 Iraq War, or with our new President from Arkansas, I was already done with the lawn. He would emerge from the house, see the whole of my work, and rarely complain. Something about the fullness and sense of completion of the work made him less likely to have any concern whatsoever. Further, my imagination tells me that something about my confidence also had a profound influence on him.

Your dissertation chair or principal advisor is like my father. If you let him see a product that is not near completed and, through your actions, say, "Hey dad, do you think this is finished yet?" the likelihood is that the answer will be "no." Instead, he will appear at the screen door of your heart, take a long-drawn-out sip of whatever, and grunt, "We need to talk about some changes to your draft." Then, from the moment you receive his premature feedback, you'll be holding two very difficult realities at the same time: First, you'll still need to complete your dissertation draft. Second, you'll also be attempting to make sense of his feedback. It's like trying to paint the side of your house while it's pouring rain — good luck. Accordingly, I recommend that you do the vast majority of your best work in "finishing" before you get your chair involved. Sure, there will be the start of the process where you need the chair to show you where the lawns are, what grass is in the first place, and how to use this mower thing. But after that, there's work to be done, and you don't need to bother the boss with it until you're pretty sure you've done the best darned job you could without his involvement. Questions will come up, but that's not the same thing as sending your chair a whole draft and asking for his opinion. Make the personal pledge that the only "drafts" that you'll send your chair are the drafts that you believe are pretty close to being finished and only need the eyes of an expert to see what you can't see. The Final Draft Pledge says, "Dr. Chair, I've gone as far with this as I can on my own using every resource open to me. Now, I'm ready for your expert eyes and feedback so that I can make the revisions required to make this the best it can be." The Final Draft Pledge is the stance of a professional and a scholar where you are bringing the best work forward because that's what's expected of you. Show your personal best. Amplify your faith in yourself and your chair's faith in you. When you get stuck, ask for help, but don't send more than what's necessary to get the help needed.

In my work with doctoral candidates, I've noticed, at times, students orienting themselves like the "sample ladies" at the big club stores in the United States who hand out free food to grocery shoppers. Candidates can get into an unfortunate cycle of asking their chairs, often by email, "What do you think about this draft?" and a few days later with some minor revisions, "How about this one?" Repeated enough times, this results in a massive time investment from the chairs in reading the candidates' work, and their faith in such candidates, at least in my experience, tends to wane. Speaking to colleagues of mine who have chaired doctoral committees, I hear that the greatest faith in students comes from their coming to the chairs for help about "specifics" when needed and help reviewing entire drafts when they are getting close (pretty darned close) to completion. The point is *not* to aim for getting a draft accepted in a single try (that's a pretty rare occurrence) but to walk as much of the road as you can as the scholar and then reach out to the experts to teach you how to climb over the final mountain. When you hand your chair your full draft of a chapter (or chapters), it should be an event — an arrival. Your draft should carry with it the confidence that you've done as much as you could on your own and that anything your chair can offer now just adds value to what you created. That's what true scholarship should feel like: Every person on the team is bringing forth his or her best to add to the depth and dimensions of the research. So, give your team great work — always. Reach out for help with specific, pointed questions.

WINNING IN YOUR INTRODUCTION

In this section, I'll show you how to conquer your introduction

and create alignment in your logic with the greatest possible ease.

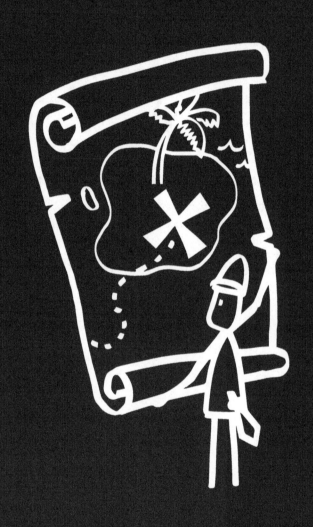

21

DOWNLOAD DISSERTATIONS
FROM YOUR PROGRAM

When I was 11, I made cookies for my parents. I consulted no book of recipes. My allies were my memory, having watched my mother make many cookies before, and my will to get this well-intentioned project finished. I found the flour, the sugar, eggs, and the butter, and began whipping them together in the way that I had seen my mother do many times before. But something was missing, and I could not remember what it was. After all, I had never made cookies before. Fortunately, I was a smart young person who felt free enough to explore the cupboard for ingredients and apply them as I saw fit. I found a bottle of brown liquid that seemed to strike a familiar chord in my memory and applied it as I felt was appropriate. A handful of minutes in the oven, and cookies were out on the rack cooling. Within 20 minutes, they were being consumed. It was only when the stomach aches began to set in for everyone who had the pleasure of eating my cookies that I realized my mistake: Apparently, instead of vanilla extract, I had added hickory liquid smoke to my cookies. In absence of a sound guide, I made everyone sick.

Today, go download five dissertations that were recently completed by doctoral students at your university. Even more specifically, download those that are from your academic program, ones that match your intended methodology, and those that were created by other students chaired by your advisor. You can take great comfort in the fact that research is built on the great work of others before you; you don't have to create the whole show. You need not engage in the guesswork of figuring out the norms of your program, chair, methodology, or university-mandated style guide. Instead, you can see what good work has been created in recent history and make some VERY informed conclusions about what needs to be addressed in your proposal draft and beyond. Further, there is a high likelihood that your university publishes a dissertation style guide or "handbook" that outlines the specifics of what is required of you and fellow candidates who are working on writing this massive text. This manual is often updated yearly by academic programs to reflect the emerging norms in their respective fields of study. With this guide and the five dissertations in your hands, you have everything you need to see the basic formatting of the document that you are about to create. Have you done this? REALLY?

ProQuest® Dissertations and Theses Global database is where I love to live when searching for research, and I hope that your university has a subscription — and I hope that this is where your university publishes its students' dissertations. If not, it's up to you to find the appropriate database that is the storehouse for individual dissertations. In some RARE cases, I've met candidates from universities where dissertations are only stored in book form. EVEN MORE RARE are candidates who have zero access to any previously created dissertations. Chances are, past dissertations from your program are stored in a digital database that is accessible to many people throughout the world. Using advanced search options, you can limit your search to your individual university. Do a blank search with your university in the institution field to find dissertations. Narrow the search to the most recent three years. Select those that are from your program. Download them. Narrow the results further in advanced search by searching for your advisor. Hopefully, your chair is listed. On your university's academic program portal or page, see if the institution offers a dissertation handbook, manual, or style guide. Download that too. In the event that you cannot access ProQuest® Research Library, call your librarian (YES, on the phone). Call your academic program office to ask if the office publishes a dissertation style guide, and inquire about how to obtain it. Print all of these documents with the expectation that you will recycle this paper in the future. On your desk, you now have the basic exemplars from which you can imagine the bare skeleton of your dissertation.

From the start, my bias is to create an individual, unified dissertation-format document. Some candidates opt to create individual chapter files or even simple double-spaced DOCX files, but I, personally, don't like the idea of having to double one's work later on. Why not create the right, singular document from the start? On those days you don't have any writing in you, would it not be useful to be able to divert your mindless attention to formatting your table of contents or appendices? First, format the blank word-processing file with the right margins. Then, start copying the dissertation format from your university-provided style guide or dissertation manual: title page, signature page, copyright page, and on and on. For the individual chapters, start looking at headings common to all the papers you downloaded, especially those that have the same methodology as yours. While the literature-review and presentation-of-findings chapters will be unlikely to provide many clues for headings, you may find your introduction, methodology, and discussion/conclusions chapters full of headings and subheadings that will be close, if not "on the way," to what will reside in your final draft. In my mind, creating a model document from the start provides numerous advantages, chief of which is being able to build the habit of creating "near-final" quality work. Further, on the many days that you will not be able to provide your best work, there are many places where you can put your attention in the ancillary components of this document. From the moment you create this document, you get to start watching the page count grow and provide something that is most palatable for your chair and committee. Be one who uses the right recipe from the moment you begin your writing.

22

NAME PURPOSE FIRST

Imagine that you are suddenly dropped on a deserted island without any food or water. You're barely clothed. The night is going to be cold. There could be wild animals here. You can see only trees for the distance of your vision. The only options are to stay on the coast or delve into the dark woods. Which would you choose? Why would you choose that option? Think about it for a minute. Often, your dissertation writing journey can be just like this. From the comfort of course-work, many are thrust into the wilderness with few allies to call on. Some doctoral students who are reading this book have *never* even spoken to their dissertation chair! Their choices are to remain where it's safe and little work is completed or, alternatively, to delve deep into the woods without any firm knowledge about what's going to happen in there. Without a goal and without the proper guiding direction, it's too easy to remain close to shore where it's safe. You may peek into the woods to see what's going on there, but it might feel too risky to go deep and to keep going, even when your brain is telling you to run like hell. Fortunately for you, with this book and some of the other books I've recommended you pick up, you have a map (or two) in hand. Still, that's not enough; you need a guiding "North" to set your sights on and to walk toward, no matter what. Define your dissertation's purpose statement (or "aim") first.

This is one of the chapters in this book where I could be in a bit of trouble as some do not agree with me on this point. Some professors will tell you, and rightly so, to do lots of reading first; then, and only then, write a purpose statement. That last part is where I disagree. I would prefer you set an intention for this study to-day. I'm 100% sure that you'll revise it in the future, so don't rigidly hold onto it. However, it's exceedingly useful, in my perspective, to create a clear and specific aim for your study. In my live workshops and in my one-on-one coaching, I walk students through this process immediately. As I duplicate it here, make sure you are doing the writing requested of you in my instructions — because there is little to no way that you'll be able to make progress by simply "thinking" the responses to my questions below. Get writing.

Who. Write a few words describing the person(s), entity(ies), or object(s) your study is attempting to better understand. For example, you might write "teachers," "companies," or "financial statements." Now, I want you to revise these words, get-ting ultra-specific. Literally, I should be able to walk into a place of your choosing and put my hand on these people or things. Can you get that specific? By this coin, you may revise your description to say "highly experienced English language arts teachers," "top consumer technology companies," or "2017 quarter-three balance sheets." The more specific you can get, the better.

Where. From the start, get ultra-specific: Where in the world can I find these people, entities, or objects? You might say "top five state-identified secondary schools in California," "top 25 Fortune 500 companies," or "publicly-traded top 10 banks in the United States." Write it down.

What. What do you want to know about these individuals, entities, or objects? Here, having some idea about a guiding theory or specific problem relating to these individuals, entities, or objects is very helpful. I'll go into more detail about this in the pages to come. However, for the sake of today, write down what you want to study. You might start with "teaching methods" but then realize that you need to get EVEN MORE specific than that. So, you might say "group-related teaching strategies." Thinking about it further, and maybe considering the mod-el or theory you're using to guide your study (if you've found such a thing), you might narrow this further to "group-interaction teaching strategies for language acquisition."

When. This is the easiest question to consider. When are you collecting your data or from what time period does your data emerge? In this case, I might write "in 2017."

How. First, choose (1) qualitative, (2) quantitative, or (3) mixed methods. Second, choose the specific methodologies that will be employed within the study. In the case of what I'm playing with here, I might say "qualitative case study."

Finally. Put it all together. Here's some of what I've been writing so far:

› *Who: highly experienced English language arts teachers;*
› *Where: top five state-identified secondary schools in California;*
› *What: group-interaction teaching strategies for student language acquisition;*
› *When: in 2017;*
› *How: qualitative case study.*

By employing the formula HOW + WHAT + WHO + WHERE + WHEN, I might come up with the following rough purpose statement:

> *The purpose of this qualitative case study is to examine the group-interaction teaching strategies for student language acquisition of highly experienced English language arts teachers at a top-five state-identified secondary school in California in 2017.*

While this will probably *not* be the final purpose statement of my (or your) study, it's headed in the right direction, and it's VERY specific. It will have the benefit of guiding your writing. What was your purpose statement? Post it to my Facebook® page! I'll do my best to send you my thoughts.

www.facebook.com/TheDissertationMentor

23

SIMPLE TO COMPLEX

The lack of specific training in logical discourse in some doctoral programs is a major disservice to their candidates. If you were to travel to many universities in the world and listen to the in-class interactions between graduate students and their faculty counterparts, you'd notice a brand of dialogue that may be strikingly missing in some academic programs. The reasons for this lack of training, as far as I see it, are threefold. First, many doctoral programs are working under an exceedingly compressed academic calendar. For instance, the prevalence of two-year and three-year doctoral degrees leaves me to wonder if some candidates truly have the time to embody the type of person who could finish a doctoral degree in the first place. I've seen it done really well in such compressed time periods; I've also seen the results of not having enough time to develop the logical, rhetorical underpinnings that allow someone to be a great researcher and academic writer. Second, the ways in which doctoral programs are choosing to interact with their students do not always match with their desires to create well-prepared, "gradu-atable" candidates. Out-of-touch online programs may leave candidates behind when they allow students to get by with substandard work or with little meaning-ful interaction with faculty. Many candidates who are reading the words on this page have never met their chair or advisor in the flesh or voice and only know this person by name and email address. Feedback to students in poorly-run programs is often cursory or nonexistent. Faculty development of candidates' capacities nec-essary for finishing a dissertation can be largely absent. Students take courses, they get grades, and they (might) meet for a couple on-ground residencies. A measure of a doctoral program's success is its ability to create well-prepared practitioners and researchers — ones who can complete the research process signified by a well-written dissertation. The final measure of a doctoral program's quality is the human qualities that it fosters in its graduates. As I said at the start of this volume, this is not about writing a paper; it's about becoming a kind of human. Finally, the last thing that I think prevents some doctoral faculty from training candidates in sound logical discourse is that professors *can* overcomplicate things. Rather than taking the time to ask candidates to bring forth the simple logic that makes up the larger reasoning for their desire to write about *this or that topic* in their dissertation, they ask candidates to go and write a 10-page concept paper. Great programs often start by asking candidates to write a single paragraph explaining what they want to study and why. My hope is that somewhere in your academic career, some educator has asked you to distill your argument, your logic down to its most essential bits. That's what I'm asking you to do here.

In the previous chapter, you were asked to create your purpose statement using the formula that I provided. My hope is that you did not trick yourself with an internal "I'll do that later" or "I've already got one" lie. Seriously, if you have not done the activity in the previous chapter, go back and do it. Please? Moving on: Create a word-processor document that looks something like this:

> *The purpose of this qualitative case study is to examine the group-interaction teaching strategies for student language acquisition of highly experienced English language arts teachers at a top-five state-identified secondary school in California in 2017.*
> [Researcher Recommendation 1]
> [Researcher Recommendation 2]
> [Researcher Recommendation 3]

Using this format, replacing the fake purpose statement above with the one that you created for your own work, it's now your turn to start looking through scholarly journal articles and dissertations to see if you can find three researchers who recommend that you study *anything similar* to that which you are saying should be researched in your study. This is not an easy request. You'll have to pore through many dissertations and articles inside your favorite research database to fulfill this request. Here's why you should do it: This truly is the most basic logic of why your study should be conducted. When you sit down with your chair or advisor to discuss your work, an important test of words will occur: Your chair will be thinking, "Is the basic logic there?" This is one of the ways (among others I'll show you in this part of the book) that you can start building that brand of simple logic.

A nightmare scenario may be awaiting you, or you may already be living it. Imagine having dozens upon dozens of pages of text and having to "align" the logic then. Imagine writing an entire literature review, 40 or more pages, only to discover that you're going to have to make massive, major revisions to the foundational logic that made up the document. Aren't sweeping revisions such as these the ones you want to ultimately minimize or avoid altogether? Revision is ALWAYS part of doctoral writing and research — always. However, by starting with the simplest argument ("I want to do this study because these three researchers say I should") and then building more and more complex lines of logic, you have a far greater likelihood of creating a document that is logically sound overall. Start super simple; then, add complexity. Only add that which logically leads to or adorns the central point of your paragraph, section, or chapter. In this case of your introduction, always logically point to your purpose statement.

24

LANDMARKS

It's not enough to have a compass and a destination; you need to know some of the perils that you'll find along the way. When I was about 10 years old, my best friend and I were visiting a lake and decided to try to walk around it. We estimated it was a small lake, and though it was going to get dark soon, we were sure we would be able to get back to the parking lot by the time the sun had gone down. Little did we know, when we made the fateful decision not to turn back halfway through our trek, that the path that surrounded the lake actually did not stick to the lakeshore the entire way. Making the foolish decision to plow forward, with the sun becoming lower and lower on the horizon, we suddenly found ourselves along unpaved service roads, under power lines, and behind gated areas of the park, all the while trying to keep the lake in sight. At one point, the trail disappeared altogether, and we found ourselves walking through thick bushes and brush. We could have been lost, hurt, or worse. Fortunately for us, persistence in our stupidity paid off, albeit we were pretty torn up from the journey. My hope is that much of this book can assist you in avoiding some of the challenges that you *don't* have to endure on the way to finishing your dissertation. It's like the Buddha said (I think): Pain is guaranteed, but suffering is optional. Knowing what's coming, specifically in your introductory chapter, is of great help. There are four landmarks that you need to create. Through this section of this book you are reading right now, my hope is that you will come away with four bullets that make up the most basic, essential logic of your dissertation. Let's start building these landmarks.

The first landmark of your introductory chapter is the "general concern" or "hook" from which your research problem and associated purpose statement will arise. Think of it this way: There are plenty of general topics in the world about which you could be concerned, about which anyone could care. Why choose this research topic? Is there something urgent or pressing that deserves our attention? This is the purpose of this landmark: to bring urgency into the conversation. So, you need to state something there that highlights information recently covered in pop media or the news about your topic. In the education world, you may say, "In a recent speech, President Obama stated…." In the healthcare world, you might say, "A recent study highlighted that only X% of people…." Whatever you say here, the result should be the same: People should read it and say to themselves, "Really? That's what's going on?" This is the diving board of your entire study, from which your readers will be jumping into the deep waters of your research. Shouldn't you at least make the dive start out interesting? Shock them with something and bring a general concern about your topic into focus.

Next, the second landmark is the "general problem." Often, candidates start out thinking that this is the actual problem that their research will be solving. Instead, they often discover that they have identified a general problem that is slightly more specific than the hook mentioned above. Based on your reading related to your topic, ask yourself, "What general problem do I see emerging out of the literature that needs to be addressed by the research?" Regularly, candidates will come forth with discussions of "We don't know…", "There is a gap in…", or "Why do…." You can fill in the blanks there. For the purpose of this section, it's important that you don't just stick to what "we don't see" in the literature, often mistakenly referred to as "the gap" (more on that later). You need to point out what the body of literature is saying "together," in unison, or how the literature is seemingly contradicting itself. This gets you from a huge topic, a large umbrella subject, into a more specific way of thinking about the topic. Instead of being about "principals," it's about "The general problem is that while we have unified standards, nationally, for assessing students' performance, no unified standard exists regarding assessing principal performance (citation, citation, citation)." With such a statement of "The general problem is…" you are taking your readers from that hulking, huge concern (the hook), the size of an entire library, down to a single shelf. Your next landmark will get your readers into a single book (also known as a dissertation).

The third landmark is the "specific problem." For this one, think now about that purpose statement that you created. Could you name three to five specific studies, dissertations, or articles that DIRECTLY ask for all or part of your purpose statement to be researched? This is part of what makes up the guts of your so-called "problem statement," which you are often naming in the latter half of your introductory chapter. If you cannot name such studies, it's your task to go and find them or change your purpose statement. Crystalize what you find into a single sentence that says something like, "The specific problem is that no up-close ethnographic accounts of nurses have been conducted in level-one hospitals in a high-crime U.S. urban environment since 9/11 (citation, citation, citation, citation)." Notice how this gets your readers so up close into the study that they can almost taste what the purpose statement is going to say. Your specific problem should do exactly that: walk your readers right next to that purpose statement (the fourth landmark of your introduction), supported by the literature, and leave them thinking, "Of course we would do a study of this kind, given the specific problem that was named." So, take out a piece of paper. Number some lines one to four. Write out your general concern, your general problem, your specific problem, and your purpose statement. You now have a four-step map of your dissertation.

25

TWENTY SENTENCES

Would you attempt to scale a 100-foot wall without the proper equipment, preparation, or training? Why, then, would you attempt to write a 100-or-more-sentence chapter of a dissertation without going through the activities that I laid out preceding this chapter? I once attempted to ballroom dance. Before our wedding, Dr. Wife and I wanted to look a little better than average on the floor during our first dance. As for me, I did not want to look like more of a hulking fool than usual. In the end, "we" decided that we would purchase a discount coupon for 12 ballroom dancing classes at a local shop. All I got from that experience was this metaphor: It's easier to learn four steps before learning the more complicated version. Quite similarly, it's easier to write your introductory chapter of your dissertation if you write the one-sentence version, then the four-sentence version, and then the 20-sentence version.

In the previous two chapters, you identified your purpose statement, doing some word-related magic, and identified the four major landmark sentences that will make up the topography of the introductory chapter of your dissertation. Here, in this chapter, I'm going to map out the actual channel through which your most basic logic will flow. If you've attempted a draft of your chapter before, you've probably heard some complaints from your professors, chair, or principal advisor about "logic" or "alignment." By following the steps I'm outlining here, I am confident that you will have a far, far better chance at having a logically aligned draft of Chapter 1. To start off, take a moment to format a Word document as you see here.

Essentially, create 20 blank lines with the sentence frames of the four landmarks present. Do your best to use these exact numbers for the time being:

1. [insert general concern here]

2.

3.

4.

5.

6.

7.

8. "The general problem is…"

9.

10.

11.

12.

13.

14.

15.

16. "The specific problem is…"

17.

18.

19.

20. "The purpose of this study…"

Using the above frames, fill in the information you created from the "four land-marks" activity in the previous chapter. Now, notice what you have in front of you. You have four sentences that have some major gulfs between them. Your task, if you choose to accept it, will be to fill up the logical gaps using *only one sentence per line*. As you try to flow from general concern to general problem, from general problem to specific problem, or from specific problem to purpose statement, there are two main principles that I want you to follow.

First, only "narrow." That is, each statement you make from sentences 2 to 7 above should only get closer to the purpose statement. Never, at least during these 20 sentences, should you side-step your logic to a side-by-side topic or point. Instead, only make a point that moves deeper toward the next intended landmark. For example, if one sentence says that nurses are underpaid, don't make the next sentence about one study that shows that nurses are underpaid. Instead, move closer to your next landmark by saying something like, "Nurses work extended, uncomfortable shifts (citation, citation, citation)." Make every sentence you create the next link in this carefully crafted chain that is getting you from general concern to purpose statement.

Second, keep the logical connection between the sentences. If in one sentence you say, "Teachers are quitting their jobs in numbers never seen before (citation, citation, citation)," it's natural to follow that with, "Numerous studies talk about the stresses of teacher life (citation, citation, citation)," followed by, "Other studies discuss the challenges of working in the public sphere (citation, citation, citation)." The intent of these 20 sentences is to provide constant, unwavering linking from sentence to sentence so that you can, in 20 sentences, describe the most basic, essential logic of your dissertation. With these guidelines, start drafting your logic such that it flows from one point to the next to the next. If the chain is unbroken, your logic will be (nearly) unshakable.

26

PROBLEM STATEMENT

Sentences 16-19 in your list of 20 sentences deserve some special attention. This is where candidates find the most trouble. After all, you probably have found much success in talking about all the background information that appears in sentences 1-15; that, by comparison, is the easy part of this chapter. However, the so-called "problem statement" section, where you name the specific, researchable problem that your purpose statement will attempt to address, remains a consistent challenge for most doctoral students. There are a couple reasons for this, at least in my experience. First, candidates during this phase of their work are required to make the most poignant, logical connections between this "interest" they've expressed in the earlier parts of their introduction and the actual study that they are planning to conduct. Simultaneously, candidates must draw *from the literature* the reasoning for why such a study should take place at all! I recall in my own doctoral studies one of my well-meaning professors saying, "Why would anyone care about this study?" Between his words and his facial expression when he uttered them, I was pretty crushed — and because of my immaturity as a researcher at the time, it caused me to walk away from my work for nearly a year. However, with the passage of time and loads of experience working with candidates, I can say now that he was right: No one cared, at least based on what I "couldn't" find in the literature, about the topic I selected. What I did not know then, and what I want to tell you now, is that the recommendations and findings of other researchers should be the guiding lights that lead you to a specific, researchable problem. Instead of some "gap" in the literature (which I took to mean "what I couldn't find") being the reasoning for doing this study, I learned as a writer, and I now teach as a guide, the specific, researchable problem is often based on three points: (1) what we know, (2) what we don't know, and (3) what researchers are asking us to find out. The gap in the literature that a study aims to address is not some void; it's the triangulation of these three points chiming in unison. The gap in the literature is a lot like a black hole in space: We can't take a picture of absence and say, "See! There is nothing there!" Instead, we have to show what's happening around the gap to illustrate what it is. So, your problem statement is made up of these three constellation points that each need to be addressed.

First, name the specific research problem that your purpose statement will address. If you have, indeed, been following along with me in the previous chapters, then you already have your specific problem ready to go.

Second, write a single sentence (item 17 in your 20-sentence list) that encapsulates *what we know* about this specific problem. Make sure to include at least three or more citations at the end of this sentence that back up what you are saying. After writing it, pause for a moment to see what you have created. Read the sentence. You should be able to say, "This is everything we know about this topic (summed up in a single sentence) that is leading me to want to do this study." Hold that in your heart for your remaining writing and for your conversations with your peers and dissertation chair.

Third, write another sentence (item 18) that sums up *what we don't know* about this specific problem. Here's where most candidates mess up by talking about "the gap" as if it were some massive extinct star in their research universe; you can't name something that's not there. What you can do is name the specific concerns, relating to your specific problem, of other researchers that they have discussed in their conclusion sections of their research. Were there startling findings in other studies that are shaking up our understanding about your specific problem? Have inconsistencies been highlighted by other researchers? Has research of this nature not been done in some time or in the intended method you have selected? Discuss, in a single sentence, all of these things that "we don't know" that are driving you to want to attack this specific problem. Support this through at least three citations.

Finally, and most importantly, name *what researchers want us to find out* about this specific problem. Here, you need to look into the recommendations for future research proposed by all those studies that you're collecting in a folder somewhere. Ask yourself, "Am I in the habit of looking at the recommendations for research as one of the ways by which I derive the reasoning and support for my study?" If you're like most candidates I've worked with, the answer is probably "no." As you are doing your readings, always take the intentional step to see what recommendations for practice and research each author makes, whether you are reading a research study or a textbook. You'll often find ample support for the brand of research relating to your specific topic (or something close) through such reading. Synthesize all that you have found into a single sentence that names what researchers are asking "us" to find out about your specific problem. Note those three or more citations.

Now, look at your purpose statement. When you read your specific problem, what we know about it, what we don't know about it, and what researchers are asking us to find out about it, do you get the sense, "Of course we would do a study like this one"? You should have that clear feeling of "Therefore, the purpose of this study is to..." being completely logically sound. You should feel like you have the confidence to go to a group of people and chat about these 20 sentences you've crafted. In fact, that's my next challenge for you.

27

TALK ABOUT IT!

At the start of my second year of my doctoral program, a research-related immersion experience was orchestrated by my university. Our first-year research professor had left the university. We were told that we would have to learn statistics without a textbook or instruction, live or via video. We were going to have to take a group test in a handful of months. If anyone in the group failed, the whole group would fail. With all of this as the backdrop of my experience with research thus far, I sat face-to-face with one of the professors of our program for a five-minute session during which I would attempt to explain my dissertation topic and receive feedback. Many of you reading this have faced this scenario: having to explain your research topic to a near stranger who has some authority inside your doctoral program. Not only did I expect to do well in this conversation, but I expected that the professor would have much acclaim for what I was going to research and offer me some helpful hints about what to do next. As you may imagine, if you have had one of these sit-down experiences or if you simply are noticing how I am setting this up on this page, my expectations were entirely wrong. I remember the feeling of tightness in my chest, like that feeling you get when your physician is listening to your heart, as I was telling this faculty member what I was planning on studying. After getting out the last breath of "...and so that is why I am planning on studying that," the face of this faculty member remained entirely unchanged — the same face of boredom he had been wearing the entire conversation. Then, something awful happened: His face curled into something far worse, which can only be described as deep skepticism and confusion. Without much explanation at all, he simply leaned in and stated with a flippant tone, "Why would *anyone* care about studying that?" And with that, and for a variety of other reasons, my dissertation work came to a complete halt — and there it remained for about 18 months.

Sitting on this side of it and having worked with so many doctoral candidates of my own now, I know that to be a doctoral researcher requires a brand of scholarly conversation and questioning in which few engage before this level of academic work. I was brought up in a church where there were right positions and wrong positions. I was brought up in a home where conflicting views were unwelcomed. I was schooled in the bath of my-way-or-the-highway classrooms through high school. I found safety in staying as silent as possible in my undergrad. All of this I have come to fully own. I had to learn, and I hope that you already have come to learn, that becoming a scholar involves questioning — and questions are actually what keep scholarship moving forward. Questions are what allow you to grow as a researcher. You need to engage daily in the art of self-questioning around your research: "Why am I researching this at all?" "Who says that this is worth researching? Why did they say that?" "What already has been researched in this specific topic? If the answer is "nothing," is it possible that I could be deeply wrong about that?" "How could I go about finding out more?" Questions like these are what allow you to make significant progress in your dissertation writing. In particular, questions like these are *most useful* at the start of the journey, when you are still trudging through drafts of your initial chapter, prospectus, or concept paper. You also need to engage in these questions with others.

As a quick side note, my experience with this faculty member in my own thin-skinned doctoral journey shows what's required of doctoral programs if administrators want to healthily raise up great scholars from their programs: They need to create the conditions for healthy conversations about candidates' research and writing. They need to coach students *and faculty members* on how to engage in these conversations. They need to prepare students for the questions that are bound to come up — particularly those that I mentioned above. Further, doctoral programs need to teach students to regularly engage in conversations with one another about what they are finding, with the acknowledgement that most students initially have little idea what they are talking about and that it's okay to still be in process of discovering the right answers (more on that later).

As for you, today, I challenge you to find a safe partner or two or three with whom you can meet regularly (perhaps every three weeks or so) via video conference for about 30-60 minutes to discuss your research. Often, it's in the small-group conversations, attempting to discuss the logic of your paper (and of the 20 sentences and problem statement mentioned in the previous chapters), where the major fruitions can take place. Record the conversations because it's often in the speaking that the logic can begin to flow. Unlike your keyboard, where the connection between your inner narrator, your brain, and your fingers can be choppy, conversation is where you can tap into a wellspring of ideas in logical sequence that you crave to get on the page. Further, it's in the honest, friendly questioning of well-meaning doctoral candidate peers that you begin to develop the skin that is able to take the licks of meetings with your chair, proposal defense, and oral defense. Some questions will floor you, but when they are asked with care and love, you can take the time to pause and consider your answers — and sometimes acquiesce to the plain fact that you simply don't have an answer. In that safety, you can learn about the holes in your logic, make a plan for discovering, and go out and prepare for the next meeting of the minds — and for the next lines to appear in your draft. Go: Talk about your dissertation to a core group of people you trust.

28

TWENTY PARAGRAPHS

When doctoral students work with me at the most formative stages of their research in The Dissertation Mentor® One-To-One Mentorship, I always ask them to forsake the urge to write their introduction and literature review until they have fully understood the logical line of argument that leads them from "the whole world" to this specific study with their specific purpose statement. In short, until you have fully worked out the purpose-statement, 20-sentences, and problem-statement approaches that I have mentioned in the chapters previous to this, I recommend *not* doing any in-depth writing of your introductory chapter. If you already have made an attempt at your first chapter, I recommend that you put it temporarily aside and start fresh with these approaches. Return to this chapter when you have completed all of the pre-work I have recommended.

With your 20 sentences in hand, you are ready to audit your logic and then catalog the supports you have amassed for each step in your logical chain leading to your purpose statement. Using your 20 sentences, follow these steps:

1. Find three different colors of sticky notes (such as yellow, blue, and green).

2. With the blue sticky notes, write out each of the four landmarks (see Chapters 24 and 25) of your introductory chapter on a separate note.

3. With the yellow sticky notes, write out each of the remaining sentences.

4. On a large wall, make a line of these sticky notes stretching from left to right, beginning with your first sentence ("hook" or "general concern"), leading to your general problem, to your specific problem, and finally to your purpose statement.

It's at this stage that you have the opportunity to see your argument lifted off the page for, perhaps, the first time. Here, you can audibly recite what you are seeing on the wall in order. Ask yourself, "To what degree does each of the sentences logically follow the one(s) before it?" Inquire of yourself, "To what degree do the yellow sentences feed the blue ones? That is, to what degree do the supporting sentences lead from hook to general problem, to specific problem, and then to purpose statement?" Consider meeting in the flesh with your small group of trusted fellow dissertation writers to conduct this exercise. With the assistance of one another, talk each other through the logic of these 20 sentences. If need be, make alterations to the sentences or adjust their order. If your logic flows without disruption, meaning that each statement leads closer and closer toward the purpose statement, you are ready now to advance to adding support:

5. Now, consider the sources that support the statement that each individual sticky note makes. For example, look at the first blue sticky note — your hook or general concern sentence. What are the sources that back up what you say in this sentence? Focus on an individual sentence and ask this question.

6. Using the final color (green), place a single sticky note under the first sentence of your line of logic. Write out a brief sentence that describes a source that supports the statement that appears above.

7. Repeat steps 5 and 6 as many times as possible until you have at least three supporting statements (on three green sticky notes) for the statement that appears above.

8. Finally, repeat steps 5-7 until every sentence of your original 20 (except your purpose statement) has at least three supports.

It's tempting during this activity to simply skip forward if you do not have the support that can back up one of the sentences of your original line of logic or if you cannot find at least three supports. Fight this urge. Look diligently — even if it takes days to do so — to find sources that support each of the sentences you place in your original line of logic. In the end, if you are not able to find such supports, that's a good indication that something may be wrong with that piece of your logic.

Once you are completely done aligning your logic with the hard work of the authors who support it, it's time, finally, to start writing:

9. Edit your 20 sentences to include citations for the supporting authors who appear below them on your beautiful sticky-note wall. For example, if the sentence that appears on the top note says, "The sky is blue," and Albert (2012), Buckly (2013), and Chin (2014) are three sticky-note supporters below, edit your original sentence to say, "The sky is blue (Albert, 2012; Buckly, 2013; Chin, 2014)." (This assumes, of course, that you are using APA® Style, sixth edition.)

10. Transfer your sticky-note masterpiece to a digital document — a hierarchical outline in your word processor including citations.

11. Finally, using this outline, begin writing your 20 paragraphs. Transform your 20 sentences, with their appropriate supports, into well-written, tightly-logical, properly cited paragraphs.

12. Go get a margarita with a friend.

29

THEORETICAL FRAMEWORK

A theoretical framework, in the most basic sense, is a map for a way of understanding the unknown. Such a framework is made up of one or more theories that may shed some light on the topic you are investigating in your dissertation. For example, Bass and Avolio's (1994) Full Range Leadership Model is a theoretical framework that combines numerous previously established theories regarding leadership and divides leadership into "transformational," "transactional," and "laissez-faire" approaches. Ken Wilber's (2000) All Quadrants All Levels (AQAL) framework combines dozens of interrelated theories into a single "theory of everything," mapping the interrelationship between what is "inside me, outside me, inside us, and outside us." In your own study, you might be examining the role of mentors of minority college professors as they made their transition from new hire to tenured faculty and, accordingly, might decide on utilizing a theoretical framework that deals with (1) mentorship, (2) the minority experience, (3) organizational leadership, or a combination of these. In short, if you consider the universe of possibility of *WHAT* you could focus on as you are collecting your data, analyzing it, discussing your findings, and relating those findings to past research, you can see that even a VERY specific study requires that you adopt a map that tells you (the researcher) where to go and why you should go there. Such a map is a "theoretical framework."

Now, here, it's a great time to discuss a closely related topic: "conceptual frameworks." A conceptual framework is a collection of closely related concepts that could be used as the backdrop, foundation, or context of your soon-to-be-interpreted study findings. Conceptual frameworks are most often used when there are no existing theories to be used to understand or shed light on what you are about to be spending the next many months (if not years) of your life understanding. Two distinct traps tend to stifle doctoral candidates at the stage where they are considering the utilization of a conceptual framework. First, it's possible that their university or doctoral program has very much misinterpreted the definition of "conceptual framework." Some universities' quality review apparatuses tell students to simply re-label their theoretical framework as a conceptual framework, even when it clearly is based on existing theory, as if these terms were simply interchangeable. I've been through a few lectures by well-meaning professors (including younger versions of myself!) who said that theoretical and conceptual frameworks are the same thing. Not true! Second, I have mentored students whose doctoral program mandated a conceptual framework be utilized in their study, even when a theoretical framework may have served them better. After all, if theories DO exist to help explain what a candidate is studying, that candidate should have the freedom to utilize such a framework for his or her study! So, the operable question that I find best for doctoral candidates to consider is this: "Can existing theories be the guiding roadmaps for understanding what I am about to study?" If yes, GREAT — you need to find yourself a theoretical framework. If no, ask yourself how this could be. Is it true that nothing out there adequately explains what you are studying? In some rare circumstances, it's possible that this is the case. However, for the most part, most candidates will probably find themselves best served by a theoretical framework.

Finding "my theoretical framework" can be an experience of awe, where you recognize the brilliance of authors, researchers, and other gifted humans before you who saw something profoundly unified about the way humans behave, the way that physics works, or the ways that the universe is seemingly chaotic yet quite poetically consistent. For me, discovering the Full Range Leadership Model, in the case of my own dissertation work, provided a road map to guide me through my continued literature search, the writing of my literature review, and the collection and analysis of my data. You are not simply looking for a theory; you are looking for a framework — hopefully something that has been drawn out, picked apart, and validated by the research of countless others. To find this theoretical framework, you have to do the hard work of searching out and reading numerous books, studies, and dissertations related to the various topics, domains, or variables that come up in your purpose statement. When you do this reading, keep an eye out for models and theories that have been employed by others to understand what they are researching. When you find a potential framework for your use, ask yourself these three questions:

1. Is this (or could this) theory or model (be) drawn out in a figure on a page? If so, draw it!

2. Is this (or could this) theory or model (be) divided into sub-domains or parts? If so, what are these parts? List them.

3. Is this theory or model applicable in the day in which we live? Alternatively, are there newer theories or models (perhaps derived from this) that would be better suited to help me understand what I am studying?

These questions will help you see the degree to which this theoretical framework is concrete enough to work with during the course of your study. Often, candidates mistakenly rely on a specific theory of whatever, not fully understanding if it is, indeed, deep enough to help them conduct their study. Remember, there will be a day when your committee will ask you, "Why did you choose this theory over others?" Will you have an answer?

WINNING IN YOUR LITERATURE REVIEW

In this section, I'll show you how "writing" your dissertation

should be the last thing you do.

30

IT'S LIKE BUILDING A HOUSE

Here in the United States, Home Depot is the ubiquitous home-improvement superstore. Any tool, hardware, gardening, or home-related item could probably be found in the dozens upon dozens of aisles. As if this were not impressive in its own right, I do attribute to Home Depot supernatural powers: It seems to have the ability to make me *always* forget the original purpose that got me through its doors in the first place. No matter if I have a list of three items for purchase or 20, I *always* forget something and find myself making a second trip back to the store. This is true enough for me and my easily distracted brain that I have kept a list now for about six years in my phone of items that I have forgotten and will need to purchase next time. A single trip back to the store takes a few hours out of my day because of where I live and the fact that I feel always compelled to walk nearly every corridor to see what amazing things have been put into stock since last time I visited. Long story short, trips cost time. Time costs energy. As long as I am "tripping," I don't get to work on the actual project that I intended to spend most of my time focusing on. Always, I would be best served by having all my materials for my projects gathered before I begin. If you were building a house, which would you prefer: (a) having all materials for the build ready to be used or (b) having to return back to the supply store each time a new part, tool, or piece of wood was needed? Naturally, everyone reading this page (unless you have been drinking again) would say that it is always preferable to have everything needed for the build *before* the building. Why, then, do students not apply this same logic to their work on their literature review?

Few doctoral candidates will be reading this page of the book without already having made an attempt at writing their literature review. The literature review, in my mind, is the greatest challenge that prevents future doctors from graduating because it requires skillsets applied over lengthy periods of time across dozens and dozens of pages. The literature review is like nothing most people have ever written. For this reason, the vast majority of The Dissertation Mentor® One-To-One Mentorship and The Dissertation Mentor® Accelerator Program have focused on getting candidates through this stage of writing. First, candidates, early in their doctoral program coursework, should establish a habit of utilizing university-provided research databases and course-mandated texts to read daily for at least 15 minutes, highlighting portions of these texts that they find compelling or applicable to their interests. Second, such candidates should select a collection apparatus to hold the quotes they have identified as noteworthy, such as Microsoft® Excel (my personal choice), Claritive Analytics® Endnote™, or Mendeley® Reference Manager (sometimes known as "Desktop," the godfather of all reference management software), and stick with it the entire duration of their study. Finally, candidates should make a personal commitment to stave off the writing of the literature review, as I have hinted at in previous chapters, until they have fully completed the process of seeking out, gathering, and synthesizing vast amounts of relevant research related to their topic. You would not start a year-long project to build a house without much research, all the building materials, and a clear plan about how you were going to use them. Again, why would you, then, start the process of writing a literature review (which could take you just as long to complete if you are not careful) unless you had conducted the expected literature search, gathered the needed notes, and had a clear plan of how you were going to go about writing this thing?

First, my suggestion is to commit, to the best of your ability, to not write much of anything in terms of a literature review until (1) you are required to do so by your program or (2) you have gathered enough materials to be able to create a full outline of your literature review. This can be challenging because candidates will equate page count with progress. Page count is not progress; it's a false idol that will lead you into destruction if you are writing without the most difficult prewriting completed. Remember that a well-built house is better than a quickly built one.

Second, develop your reading habit today. Reading is progress. "Progress" is your personal, developing understanding of the various domains you are researching. Your ability to have a scholarly conversation with your professors and peers about theory and theory-informed practice is progress. Read for at least 15 minutes per day and highlight those portions of text that are of interest to you or seem to build on other ideas you have noted before.

Finally, start cataloging those items that you have highlighted. Make the commitment from the start to only keep notes that include full citations in the format selected by your university (APA, MLA, etc.). Imagine that there will come a day when coursework ends and you have 400 notes ready to be employed in your writing while others around you have none. Imagine the inverse, where you have nothing to show for all your reading over the past years. Which seems most wise? Start reading, start highlighting, start cataloging. Remember always: Progress is understanding, not pages.

31

THEORY AREAS

Another formative episode of my doctoral experience was participating in a team presentation of the history of a theoretical domain. In my team's case, because I was studying education and organizational leadership at the time, we were required to present the history of leadership, starting back, *way back*, in history, leading to the present. I was responsible for two sections of the presentation: leadership in antiquity (ancient times) and leadership in the post-postmodern age. This project most satisfied me as a learner as I gained experience in scholarship I had never been exposed to prior: I learned the developmental steps that humans took to understand and employ leadership throughout time. It was in this experience that I learned one of the most important capacities as a scholarly practitioner: to see how my work as a researcher should build on the good work of other scholars who came before me. As a young dissertation writer undertaking this mini-literature review and presentation, I learned that I was not alone in my work and that everything that I could want to do as a researcher would spring forth from the foundational work, observations, practice, and scholarship of others. I learned that I was going to have to do LOTS of reading and learning to be able to conduct a literature review.

Quite similarly, you too are going to have to learn so much to be able to conduct your initial literature search and undertake a full review of the literature. It's not enough (or even wise) to hunt for and find single pieces of writing worthy of citation to insert into your working draft, as if you were building that house I discussed in the last chapter one stick at a time. First, you must acknowledge that there is a whole world of scholarship about the various domains that your study touches. So, let's start there: Let's talk about "theory areas" or domains.

A domain of knowledge (or simply "domain") is an area of human endeavor around a certain discipline. For dissertation work, when working with doctoral candidates, I often choose to call these domains of knowledge "theory areas," as it helps them understand that they are going to research theories within a few specific disciplines for the purposes of their own scholarship. For example, if you are studying leadership, you'll come to understand the various stages of development of that human practice and scholarship within this theory area — you are going to learn the history of the theories, practices, and research of leadership. In the case of nursing education, you're going to learn the theories, practices, and research that make up the history of nursing education. For your study, what theory areas apply? Take a look at your purpose statement. For example, let's take this fictional purpose statement:

> *The purpose of this qualitative case study is to examine the curriculum design practices of high school principals at highly effective California public secondary schools during 2017.*

First, highlight or underline all the possible theory areas within your purpose statement; that is, highlight all those terms that could be searched in a research database or could have a book titled *The History of [insert theory area here]*. In the case of this purpose statement, it could look like this:

> *The purpose of this **qualitative case study** is to examine the **curriculum design practices** of **high school principals** at **highly effective California public secondary schools** during 2017.*

For the time being, leaving out the methodology named at the start of the purpose statement, you can see that at least three theory areas are defined according to this purpose statement: (1) curriculum design practices, (2) high school principals, and (3) highly effective California public secondary schools. What theory areas emerge from your purpose statement?

Additionally, it could be said that there is a fourth theory area hidden within the purpose statement, which is a combination of all the terms. For example, the fictional purpose statement also has a theory area called "the curriculum design practices of principals at highly effective California public secondary schools." This fourth theory area acknowledges that you will sometimes be examining documents related specifically, *only* to the theory, practice, and research of "curriculum design practices." Other times, you may find something that relates to *both* "curriculum design practices" *and* "high school principals" at the same time. Accordingly, you need a mental space (and a space within your citation manager and literature review) to hold such "combo" tidbits of information.

With your theory areas named and in hand, you are ready to start delving into the research databases and other library resources to see what exists out there related to the terms with which you are working. It's at this stage that I highly recommend scheduling time with your school's librarian to get an introduction to the research-related resources that are available to you. Believe it or not, a human being is most likely paid by your university to help you get started in your research. Ask the librarian if the university does interlibrary loans. Ask the librarian if he or she can, for free, ship books directly to your home or inbox. Ask the librarian if the university has access to ProQuest® Research Library. If it doesn't, ask the librarian if he or she could get you access to this amazing resource. Schedule some time with the librarian to help you learn about the library and what it offers.

32

GET DISSERTATIONS FIRST

As evidenced by my experience with candidates in my coaching programs, doctoral programs *may* be overemphasizing the importance of obtaining journal articles at the formative stages of one's doctoral journey. Though it's clear that no doctoral student will finish his or her dissertation if he or she does not access hundreds of journal articles, in my opinion, it's not the best place for candidates to start. As I indicated earlier in this volume, the best place to begin is with dissertations from your own program (see Chapter 21), especially those published recently in your own methodology, so that you can see what the expectations are from your own program. The reasons you want to access dissertations early in your process are simple to understand: (1) To write a dissertation, you'll want to be a reader of dissertations; (2) dissertations have these amazing things at the end of them called "reference lists," where you can learn about all the resources that the researchers used for the purpose of their scholarship; and (3) dissertations end with recommendations for research and practice that often can establish the basis for doing your own study. After all, it's nice to do a study when other researchers are telling the world that such a study should be done.

Additionally, I already described how to utilize dissertation research databases to look for dissertations emerging from your doctoral program and, hopefully, those related to your dissertation chair or advisor as well. Here in this chapter, it's time for you to begin the process of amassing a collection of dissertations that are related to the various theory areas of your study. Start by getting a piece of paper (turned horizontally) or opening up a fresh Microsoft® Excel spreadsheet. Write all of your theory areas along the top line. Building off the previous example, you could have the following:

curriculum design practices | *high school principals* | *highly effective high schools*

Next, do a search (searching "full text" options only, if possible) within your dissertation database of choice (again, see Chapter 21) by placing one of your theory areas inside quotes. For example, you could search for "curriculum design practices." Note how the quotes ensure that the full term of "curriculum design practices" is searched rather than "curriculum" AND "design" AND "practices." You are only looking for anything that matches all these terms together. Ask yourself, "How many results did I obtain?" Make a note somewhere of the search terms and the number of results. Next, look at some of the abstracts or descriptions appearing for these dissertations. Do you see any patterns regarding word choice? Is it possible that "instructional design practices" may be a more widely accepted term for the same theory area? Add it to your page or spreadsheet as a synonym, like this:

curriculum design practices | *high school principals* | *highly effective high schools*
instructional design practices

Run a search for your newly chosen synonym. How many results did you obtain? Often, it's at this stage that you may see that your new search term may relate to a different theory area altogether or that it warrants further investigation to understand the relationship between the two search terms you have selected. Repeat this process and amass a list of as many synonyms as you feel are appropriate for *all* your theory areas. Overall, your goals are to (1) understand the constellation of search terms that may relate to each theory area, and (2) discover what specific search term is the most widely accepted, named expression of each theory area. For example, you'll find with closely related terms, like "teaching," "instruction," and "facilitation," that generally one search term is more widely accepted than the others. Always gravitate toward the most popular and appropriate search term based on what you are studying.

Next, now that you have the most widely accepted search term for each theory area and the most prevalent synonyms for each, it's time to start doing some combination searches. For example, for my mock purpose statement, I might search for

"instructional design practices" AND "high school principals"

"instructional design practices" AND "principals"

"curriculum design practices" AND "principals"

"instructional design practices" AND "secondary schools"

"instructional design practices" AND "secondary schools" AND "principals"

You may even choose to limit your searches (if there are enough dissertations populating your university's own database of finished candidates) to your university, program, or chair/advisor.

As you perform your searches and see your results reducing from 16,000 to 1,000 to 16, you'll have much greater success in locating those dissertations that are most closely related to your own. You'll find loads of reference lists that can give you clues as to what articles, books, and dissertations you may wish to access to better understand each of your theory areas. You'll find exemplary dissertations that show you what is possible in this mode of scholarship. You'll also find recommendations for future research that will be very useful in establishing the ground for your own study. Go forth and read!

33

GET BOOKS

There is a needless taboo in doctoral programs, circulating among students, regarding the utilization of books within their literature review. Some professors overemphasize the importance of the contributions of peer-reviewed academic journal articles to such a degree that students think that books are completely off limits. In some doctoral programs, I have heard of faculty members banning the utilization of books within a literature review altogether (though this is rare). Peer-reviewed texts of all kinds, regardless of whether they have a hard-cover binding or exist as a 20-page PDF file online, are useful in conducting your literature review. However, it's worth noting that each type of text plays a very specific role in your review. For example, in the previous chapter, I talked about how dissertations are useful for finding great exemplars of the type of document that you are writing, finding sources to study for your own literature review, and seeing the recommendations for future research. To summarize, I see various types of sources as having very different roles in your quest to understand each of your theory areas. Here are these roles, in the most basic sense:

1. Dissertations: Illustrate what this document could look like and how the process of writing a dissertation (and conducting the associated study) is carried out; provide recommendations for future research; provide a convenient list of potential reading materials via the reference list.

2. Books: Define, describe, explain, and analyze history, theory, and epochs of practice; critique history, theory, and practice; provide a forum wherein, at length, seminal authors can outline, distinguish, analyze, and synthesize the culmination of their research (and the research of others) into a cohesive presentation.

3. Journal articles (which could, among many other examples, include the presentation of a study, literary analysis, or book review): Present the most state-of-the-art scholarship to date; provide recommendations for future research; provide a forum for seminal, established, and emerging scholars within their fields of study.

You can see from this list that books provide an interesting opportunity for you to learn about the history of your theory areas, hear from the most defining voices (potentially) within a specific domain of knowledge or scholarship, and gain an understanding at a highly critical and evaluative level. Many books are written from a top-down approach, where the logical argument can be developed over hundreds of pages. This differs significantly from the way in which study results are published in journal articles, where only a handful of pages may be dedicated to understanding the historical, theoretical, and practical underpinnings of the scholarship. Ask yourself, "Would books or journal articles help me better understand the history and theory when I am at my most formative stages of understanding?" I admit I'm setting you up for a specific answer here: I want you to name one of your theory areas, get on the university's library web page, reserve 20 books, and get them into your hands. I want you to do this because I know that once you start delving into those books, you'll drop the superficial way of seeing the subject about which you are reading. I know that you'll start experiencing each of your domains of study more and more as a scholar, letting go of the web of anecdote, rumor, and flawed logic that can often make up our understanding of our daily work in any area of knowledge. As one of my mentors used to say, it was conventional wisdom as a teacher 30 years ago to not smile until the second or third month of instruction, lest the children think you're a pushover. It sometimes takes a summative look at an area of study to understand what's happening within it. Often, books can provide those tasty overviews or, at least, provide a snapshot of a particular time in the history.

Books have their place in your scholarship. Truly, there is nothing wrong with accessing a book called *The History of Nursing Training* to understand the history of the training of nurses. However, do note that this book cannot be the end of your scholarly journey. Journal articles will have their place too. You *will* end up accessing many a journal article about nursing training (or whatever) during the course of conducting your literature review. Books, though, offer something that many journal articles do not: a profound physical presence within your workspace. They are, unless you opt for an online version, bulky, smelly, imposing monoliths on your desk that will psychologically hound you until you do something with them. They become, in and of themselves, checkmarks of progress as you are able to return books that you have cataloged, read, noted, and digested. Further, they literally put in your hands the way by which you are knowing if you are doing dissertation work: If you are not holding a book in your hands every 24 hours or so, you know that you are not making progress, are putting off your future happiness, and are allowing the forces of darkness to win — and who wants that? So, call your librarian; *YES, call this person*! Tell your librarian what you are researching and ask him or her to help you find 10 great books about one or more of your theory areas. Ask your librarian if the library provides a shipping service whereby he or she can send you materials to your home. Get books into your hands, on your desk, and into your private dissertation writing space. Allow them to do the work of staring you down until you pick them up and show them some love.

34

FIVE TIMES FIVE

Great things come from many small things. Often, we can become so enamored of (and overwhelmed by) the gravity of our goals that we lose the perspective of the day-to-day and, often, moment-to-moment actions that truly make up the effort that will ensure our aspirations come to fruition. When I was teaching high school, students who were living deeply troubled lives would often express their goal to graduate, a great thing by any standard! Still, in my own observation, they were always best served simply by doing better today (right now) than yesterday. If they *fully* understood what was going to be required of them to finish their high school work, they would be much more likely buried under the massive requirements of this undertaking. However, when I would say, "Your task during this next 50 minutes is to not let anyone get you so angry that you can't read anymore," "Your job for the next 10 minutes is to read this page while being the least distractible you can be," or "Spend two minutes rewriting this sentence with the handwriting of a man who wants his words to be readable by his grandchildren," students were always more able to fulfill these tasks. The "scale" of these tasks was sufficiently small to allow progress. Quite similarly, you may be overworking yourself already in your life. Accordingly, the prospect of taking on a whole dissertation (even if you fully understood what that meant from start to finish) is too much. Instead, you can reduce the scale of your daily dissertation work to such a level that it's (1) workable, doable, and solely a matter of putting the time and brain matter toward the task, and (2) clear if the tasks were completed or not. You should be able to walk away with a number, being able to say something as plain as, "I skimmed one book today," or "I gathered five great quotes today."

In the "Chunk It" section of this book (Chapter 18), I talked about keeping like tasks with like tasks. Here, I want to give you a very specific method for conducting your literature review, or at least gathering many of the materials that will make up the guts and sinews of the analysis, synthesis, and evaluation that you are going to be eventually doing. As a matter of pre-work, my hope is that you've taken my advice about reaching out to your school's librarian and spending some time with this person physically or via phone. If you've not done this, it makes me wonder why you've decided not to. Do you have some internal bias against working alongside experts in the library sciences? Do you hate librarians? Do you hate telephones? Further, I hope that you've gotten about 10 or more books into your hands, spread throughout the various theory areas under exploration. Here is a summary of what I would like you to have in hand as you undertake the activity to follow:

1. 10 or more dissertations in which, perhaps, you've found useful lists of other resources so that you are able to find

2. 10 or more journal articles and

3. 10 or more books related to one or more of your theory areas.

If you don't yet have these, please stop reading and go about finding these resources. Once you have these, it's time for you to learn the "five times five" literature-reviewing method.

First, pick up a journal article or book. Grab a highlighter or a set of sticky notes and begin by skimming the layout of the text. If applicable, look at the table of contents, chapter headings, and other section markers. While doing this, utilize your tools to mark areas of the text that seem of interest or applicable to what you are studying. Remember to generalize your approach. If you are looking into the "mentorship of African-American faculty members in higher education," you'll be looking for many things including mentorship, African-Americans, faculty, and higher education.

Second, once you have flagged those sections worth examining, it's time to start skimming. "Deeply skim" your sections of interest, looking for materials that are of interest to you. By deeply skim, I mean a healthy balance between blazing-speed, clumsy skimming and all-in reading. You probably won't have enough time to read the text in depth. However, you don't want to waste the chance to stay awake and actually find useful materials. When you come across a quote worth noting, highlight it or flag it with one of your sticky notes. Don't pause your skimming process for more than a few seconds to accomplish this. Remember that you are chunking your activity, not stopping every time you find something useful. Keep reading until you finish the source.

Finally, make a point to find at least five useful quotes from your chosen text and transfer these notes to your software of choice. In 99% of cases, you'll find something worth quoting within all the sources that you obtain, save the time that you end up with a book about dolphins when you are studying educators. In the event that a chosen quote actually cites others (your author cited another author), I suggest making a note of that source and putting it on your list of future items to obtain.

Now, repeat this five-quote-hunting process with a total of five sources for your sitting session for the day. If successful, you'll have 25 quotes (five quotes times five sources) entered into your software platform. Now, call, text, or turn to a friend and say, "Hey, I got lots done on my dissertation today! I skimmed five sources and got 25 useful quotes!" Feel accomplished. Get some sleep. Have dreams about the future. Repeat it again tomorrow.

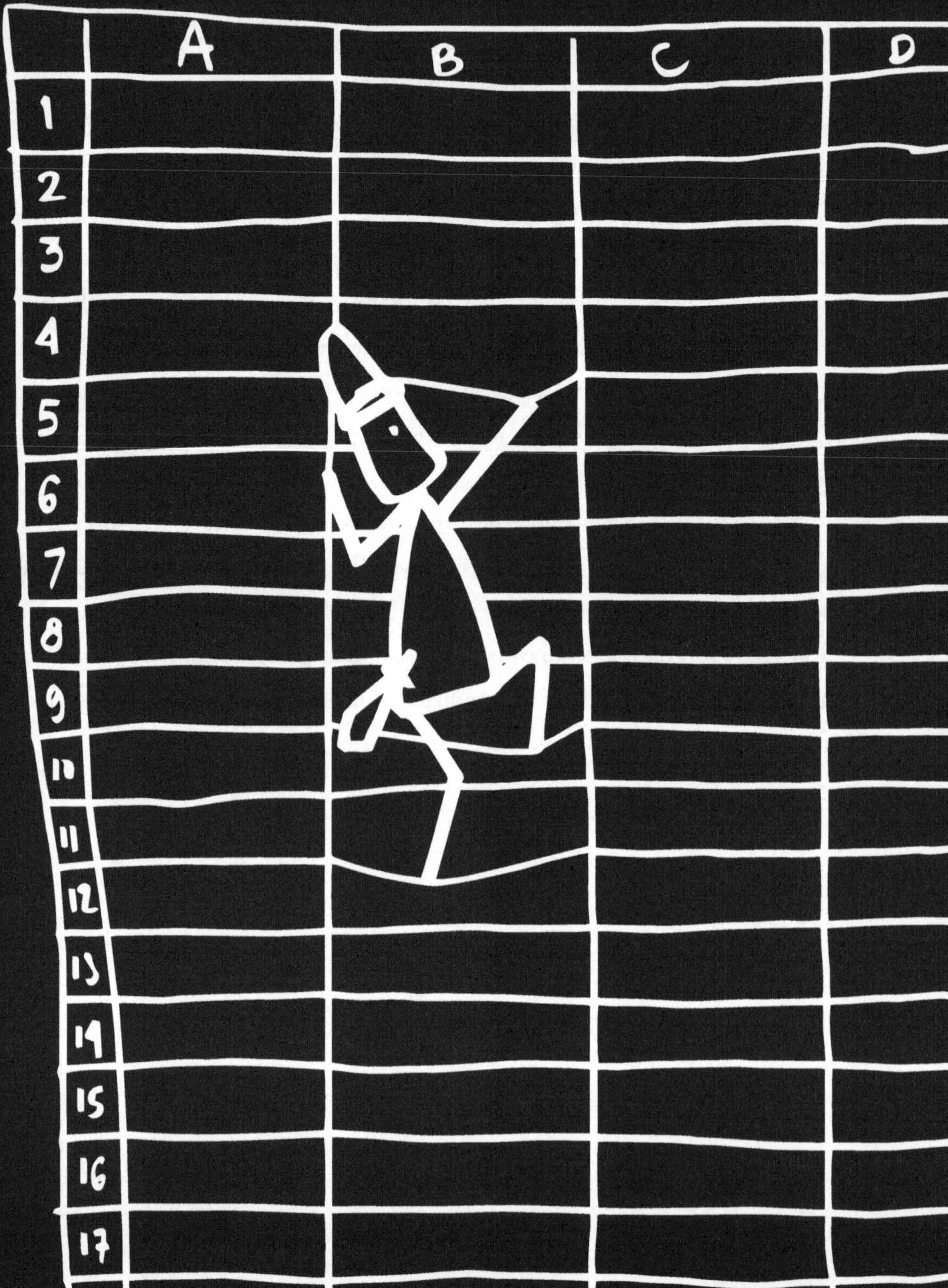
A
B
C
D
1
2
3
4
5
6
7
8
9
10
11
12
13
14
15
16
17

35

MATRIX

You need a way to catalog all the quotes of interest that you encounter in the months and years leading up to the writing of your literature review. Remember: The physical product in page count called a "literature review" is really the result of a process called "reviewing the literature." That is, it could take months or years to have all the materials required to complete your review. If you are fortunate, or motivated, you can start this journey early on in your doctoral work. You can read, flag sections of importance, highlight or mark quotes of interest, and transfer these notes into some sort of system to collect these quotes. Usually, I get three questions that emerge out of this:

1. Why quotes? Am I really supposed to be using quotes in my writing?
2. How many quotes do I need to collect?
3. What do you mean by "system" used to collect my quotes?

I'll get the first two questions out of the way right away. Then, I'll spend the rest of this chapter addressing the third.

Why quotes? Rarely in your actual writing will direct quotes (where you type the actual words of your sources with "quotes" around them) appear. This, perhaps, was suitable for undergraduate work, but in the doctoral world, we're looking for deeper understanding than simply regurgitating what others have said. You're going for high levels of understanding called "synthesis," "application," and "evaluation" (more on that later). The reason I want you to collect quotes, as opposed to making paraphrased notes about what you find, is that you *rarely* will be able to re-obtain an original source once you read it, annotate it, and transfer notes into your collection system. So, would I rather you have a copy of paraphrased notes or the original quote when separated by six months or more of time and a six- to 12-week delay in getting the source material back into your hands? You may never hold a source in your hands again; wouldn't it be nice to know exactly what it said instead of what you thought it said? This is why you collect quotes: Not because you are going to quote directly in your final writing but because you want to preserve the original intent of the source.

Next, it follows that I am always asked, "How many quotes do I need to collect to conduct a literature review?" This is a difficult question to answer, as the length of literature reviews differs from school to school and program to program. However, I can throw out some common numbers that I have seen. I offer no guarantees that these will be the numbers for you, but they point to the gravity of what will be needed in your research. For EACH of your theory areas that you name through your purpose statement, it's common to have 100-150 quotes minimum, on average (in my limited experience). This assumes that you have adequate historical, theoretical, and practical coverage in your quotes, spanning the timeframe that you are investigating. For example, if you have 25 quotes covering the 1970s and only two quotes covering the 1980s, you can see that more research will be required on your part. The point is not really the numbers (though the numbers help illustrate how much work you will be doing at minimum); the point is that you need to cover the timeframes necessary to show the story of the history, theory, and practice for each of your theory areas from the past to the present (more on that later).

Finally, the point of this chapter of this text: You need a system to catalog your quotes. A stack of books and paper two meters high in your office space with highlighted pages does you little good in the days to weeks that you will spend outlining and writing your final draft of your literature review chapter. You need some way to keep track of what quotes you have amassed. Further, you need some way of measuring your daily progress while you are conducting your literature search and review. As mentioned before, there are a number of software options you could employ. You decide what's best. However, I prefer Microsoft® Excel, as it's simple: boxes and text. That's it. No learning curve. No special online syncing that could go bad. It's just me and a spreadsheet. I recommend trying out this simple approach first before using specialized software. Start by creating a file with the following column headings: year, source, theory area, sub-theory area, and quote. Today, do your five-times-five process defined in the previous chapter of this text. Write all 25 of your quotes on separate lines. Yes, you will be copying and pasting certain details, like the year and source of the quote, throughout your lines. When you are done, look at the screen. Take a deep breath. You now have 25 more quotes than you had yesterday. Tomorrow, if you hit 50, you are making great progress. Notice how you now have a single way by which you can track your literature-reviewing progress? Notice how all your work appears in one place such that you can start seeing connections between the lines appearing? Notice how you can use the "sort" feature to sort quotes by theory area, by sub-theory area, and by year? Want to measure your progress in each theory area? Simply do a sort and see how many quotes appear for each decade or for each sub theory area. You are not reliant on browsing through many screens and performing many clicks to see all the hard work you have done; it's right in front of you with this approach. I refer to this spreadsheet as your "matrix." Go now and create yours. Let it be the place where progress is measured and in your face each day.

36

HISTORY. FAMILIARITY. EXPERTISE.

Imagine for a moment you are at the dentist's office. Your mouth is open under those big lights. The dentist and her assistant are prepping to do some work on your teeth — the type of work that you would prefer not to do but will do for the sake of your health and well-being. The dentist peers into your mouth, pauses with a bewildered look, and retreats to a countertop behind you where she has a *Beginner's Dentistry* book open on the table. She starts to read, pointing her latex-tipped finger on the page, murmuring, "Hmmmmm...." Does this inspire confidence within you as her patient? If she were to return to your mouth, tool around in there for a bit, and then retreat back to that textbook, repeating this process over and over, would this make you feel as if you could trust her? Think about the product of her work: Do you feel that the product of her work will be better or worse based on her need to constantly return to the text before fiddling around inside your jaw? Quite similarly, your own need to be typing in a Microsoft® Word document called "Literature Review" while reading a single book, journal article, or dissertation should spark within you a feeling of unease. If you are typing directly into your doctoral dissertation document whilst reading a book from which you are lifting text, something is deeply wrong. You are skipping to surgery before learning about surgery or making a plan for the surgery. You are learning to fly a plane without lessons or plans. You are making yourself into that acquaintance who speaks with supposed expertise, when in reality, this person has nothing worth saying at all. Don't become such a person. Become the expert before you write.

When chairing an oral defense, I always use the same line that my own dissertation chair used with me as I entered mine: "We are here to listen to the expertise of [insert your name here]. S/he is the expert of this study, and we are looking forward to having a scholarly conversation with him/her about what s/he has learned." If you work very hard, there will come a day when you too will sit in this seat of expertise. However, you can't fake your way there — or, at least, few can, and those who do never finish their doctoral journey. You can't fake your knowledge of history, your familiarity with your areas of study, and the expertise that you have developed. Through your reading, you are not solely looking to "write a literature review" or "collect X quotes" or "say just the right things to make your chair happy." These things don't, in and of themselves, produce the transformation that you will have to experience to successfully defend your dissertation. You have to develop three capacities that can only arise through true practice and discipline, true reading, and informed, well-planned-out writing.

First, you need to develop an understanding and appreciation for the complex histories of each of your theory areas. You need to find authors who discuss the periods that make up the history of a specific domain of knowledge. You might find that the history of public education in Australia has five specific time periods, or four, or three, depending on what authors you come across. You might discover that the history of post-postmodern cyber-security has distinct time periods that are closely related to the individual geopolitical conflicts that arose in the world throughout the past 40 years. Even more deeply, you need to know the big names, and a few of the smaller names, that arose within each time period associated with each period of development for each of your theory areas. If you are an educator, you'll hear the names Vygotsky, Piaget, and Bandura. In other fields, you'll learn other names. You'll learn about the historical events that moved each theory area from one time period to another. You'll learn the voices of theory, research, and practice that emerged throughout each moment. You will be able to tell the story of the history of each of your theory areas invoked by your study.

Second, you need to develop familiarity with the theoretical and practical approaches to each of your theory areas. You won't simply know that psychologists were concerned at one point in history with strengthening the ego; you'll understand what ways of seeing the world contributed to psychology's focus on strengthening the ego. You will, more and more through your reading, be able to put yourself into the shoes of the researchers, practitioners, and laypersons who lived through each period of development for each of your theory areas. You'll understand the essential assumptions with which they were living. You'll understand what made them tick. You'll learn the questions they were asking, what answers they discovered, and how these answers changed the landscape of theory and practice.

Lastly, you need to develop the approach of an expert — one who has made a careful study of a domain of knowledge and can speak readily about its complex landscape of history, theory, and practice. You need to develop the level of expertise required to reflect on this landscape from a 30,000-foot perspective and be able to zoom in and provide a critique of what happened, when it happened, what was known, what was not known, what researchers wanted us to know, and what we humans found as a result. It's not just that you are going to understand how one theorist, researcher, or practitioner approached a question of his or her time; you need to develop the expertise to understand the relationship between these experts' questions and the questions of their time — and what was found, and what new questions sprung forth. Truly, the only way to build such expertise is with time and dedicated focus. So, read and take notes as if your finished dissertation depends on it.

37

WHAT DO RESEARCHERS WANT US TO FIND OUT?

When that faculty member was staring at me blankly, unimpressed with my emotional fervor about my dissertation topic, I failed to realize that the best scholarly support for any notion, line of logic, topic, purpose statement, or significance of a study is the recommendations of other researchers. That is, I did not have to invent the support for my study by cobbling together a mix of my heart's desires and biases with some logic sprinkled in here and there. Instead, all I had to do was keep my eyes open from the early start of my reading during my literature search and review process. After all, authors time and time again were bringing forth their recommendations for future research and practice. However, I rarely focused on those words. Often, when I work with doctoral candidates, I see them focusing on the initial setup of the logic in other researchers' opening paragraphs or the results of their studies or exposition. Rarely do candidates take note of what these researchers, through their hard work, recommended for future research.

Take stock of the journal articles related to research studies and dissertations that you have amassed thus far. How many notes have you taken on the recommendations for future research contained within those documents? Can you point to support for your *own study* using the recommendations for future research presented by others? So many candidates will support the significance of their own study with pathos or ethos. That is, they communicate their passion about a topic through nonsense words (at least in research writing) such as "imperative," "important," "crucial," and the like. Alternatively, they write from the perspective of

"Should we not be asking questions like these?" or "These are the questions worth asking," without providing the logical backing to support such a position. A logos approach, wherein you cite evidence for your arguments, is the strongest, and largely the only acceptable, way to write in a dissertation. You need an evidentiary, logical way to support your study. It's not just an idea you like. It's not that it's an idea that you think is important (or even that others seem to highlight as "vital"). You need to find the words of others that directly recommend that your study (in part or in full) be conducted. If the evidence led them to make such a recommendation and you are fulfilling such a call for research, then you are forwarding the work of scholarship and practice. That seems significant to me! In fact, you probably are being asked to talk about the significance of your study, and what better way could you discuss the significance of your study than by showing how it forwards the work of scholarship and practice? Chances are, you already have skimmed past *golden* recommendations by researchers in your field. So, you need to keep your eyes open, go back, and see if those who have researched before you have left breadcrumbs of logic leading right up to the support for your study for which you have been looking!

In your literature matrix that you have begun amassing, I personally recommend that you create a special tag or "sub-heading" specifically related to recommendations for future research named by texts with which you interact. In my own writing practice, I keep a special column called "notes" where I can put the words "recommendation for research" as a unique marker that can be sorted within Microsoft® Excel. I could sort by notes, then theory, then sub-theory, then year to see a chronological list of every recommendation made by researchers in each of the domains discussed in my study. There are numerous advantages to this. First, I can see the history of the questions with which researchers have been grappling over time. I can see the ways in which various discoveries of many researchers led to deeper and deeper understandings — and more questions that rolled forward. This is one of the most exciting things to me about research: It's not about authority telling us what is true. All researchers worth the ink on their pages are held to the standards and rigors of peer review, just as you will be in a handful of months or years. What makes something worth dissertating on is that the questions are worth something. People have pointed to the questions you're considering and said, "THIS! *This* is what we need to learn!" That's very exciting. Second, you can recognize that the types of questions researchers ask are often the result of the context of their times, locations, and levels of consciousness. The questions that permeate your organization are also the result of these. The questions you *personally* consider are the result of your context and your anchoring stage of development as a human being. At a point in the near future, when you sit and defend your dissertation, you should be able to discuss each of the stages of development of each of your theory areas. Start writing down the questions with which researchers have concerned themselves. Then, write down the further recommendations for research that have emerged from their findings.

Next time you speak to your chair about your dissertation topic, I challenge you to speak from your knowledge of what other researchers have asked you to research. Say things like, "Walter (2010) recommended that research be conducted about…. James (2013) said we need to learn more about…and Jenning (2014) called for an examination of…. THEREFORE, the purpose of my study is to…." You should have the confidence to simply be able to say that you saw that the researchers are hungry for a specific type of food and that you, accordingly, will be satisfying them by making what they are asking for.

38

FOUR-BOX LITERATURE REVIEW

Multitasking is the death of your writing process. If you want a way to guarantee that you will make little or no progress in your writing, simply open up a Microsoft® Word document in one window, open up a browser window in another window, and start searching for items to integrate live into your working draft of your literature review. Nothing good can come from that because switching between searching, refining your search, finding the document, downloading it, opening it, reading it, finding something worth your time in it, typing a quote or paraphrasing into your own draft, and integrating it into the line of logic that you are developing — all of which you are attempting to complete within a handful of minutes — subjects you to too much at once. It's like trying to do math while someone sits next to you shouting random numbers into your ear. Wouldn't it be easier and more worth your time to do one type of task at a time? If you were at the supermarket trying to decide on a recipe for dinner, who would attend your dinner, and how you would invite them all to dinner; looking for all the ingredients; and minding all the food preferences and allergies of your attendees while also talking on a cell phone, not knowing your way around the store, would you not think that there would be a more organized way to have a dinner party? Why, then, do so many candidates do this to themselves when they are conducting their literature review? The most organized way, the best policy, is to take one research step at a time. This is primary school stuff, when your teacher told you that you should outline before you write. I am imploring you to make the commitment to do your writing last. Specifically,

I'm asking you to conduct your literature review in four steps.

There are four primary tasks, or "boxes," that I see as making up your process of conducting your literature review:

1. Finding and retrieving sources;
2. Qualifying and flagging sources;
3. Reading, annotating, and drawing quotes from sources; and
4. Returning and filing sources.

These tasks should be completed separately . For the collection of readers and coaching clients with whom I work who only have 15-30 minutes a day to dedicate to their dissertation work, I recommend that they only complete one of these steps per sitting. Dedicate 15 minutes to finding and retrieving sources, and call it a day. Spend the next day qualifying and flagging sources, and so on. Others may complete the four tasks in 45-minute segments. In my own writing practice, I do a 45/15 split of each hour. I'll spend 45 minutes on finding sources and then take a 15-minute break, walking around the roads that surround my office space. I'll spend the next 45 minutes qualifying and flagging sources. Then, I'll spend about 15 minutes dancing like a fool in the room adjoining my office. I'll then spend 45 minutes reading, annotating, and drawing quotes from sources. Then, yes, you guessed it, I'll take a 15-minute break. I repeat this process over and over again so that I can achieve the highest degree of speed and focus within each individual task. I stay within each "box" of a limited number of tasks as long as it's beneficial to me. Then, I move on when I'm exhausted, bored, or needing a change of pace. NEVER will I move into another type of task during my time in one of these boxes. Let's go through each of the boxes in a small amount of detail so that you can employ this today.

First, when finding and retrieving sources, you probably will have a browser window open to your university's library web page. You might have a specific research database up. You'll refine your search terms, as I described in a previous chapter, and download PDF files of every resource that seems like it may be a match for that which you are searching. Don't read much of anything in this stage.

Stick to finding and retrieving only. In one sitting, you may download 50 PDF files of journal articles or dissertations. You might reserve 25 books at your university's library that you'll run by and pick up tomorrow. You might have placed requests for 10 books via interlibrary loan that could take a few weeks to obtain. Notice how this first "box" is an "inbox" step. You are getting materials into your inbox, on your desk, into a file folder on your computer. Pause. Don't start the next box until you are done with this initial one.

Second, qualify and flag resources by asking two simple questions. Pick up one source, a single document, and ask, "Is this something worth reading?" If you are learning about teachers and you accidentally downloaded something about penguins, you have your answer! Put down the document and move on. If it is something worth reading, then ask yourself, "What in this is worth reading?" Start skimming the table of contents, headings, table names, bolded text, recommendations for future research, and other notable sections. Simply skim. With a highlighter or sticky note, flag those sections worth further reading. Pause here. Your work for the day may be done.

Next, read the sources one at a time. Copy quotes worth noting into your literature matrix.

Finally, make your spouse and officemates happy by clearing your desk of all the materials you have processed. File them or return them. This is your outbox.

39

FIVE TIMES FIVE TIMES 20

Largely, I see two options in front of dissertation writers. The first option is to go the conventional path of many doctoral candidates, slogging through draft after draft without feeling the joys of progress, spending much of their time attempting to jump to the final part of the writing process, finding themselves unable to write the final product they so desire to complete. In a way, such candidates are often drawing forward the same writing habits they have always held. They say things to themselves like, "I don't need to annotate sources, gather quotes, synthesize them in a spreadsheet or matrix, and outline a few times before writing; I can game the system and jump to writing the same way I always have!" Doctoral students in this mindset, the one that ignores the "process" part of writing process, often stew in ABD agony for years. I don't want you to have a bad case of ABD! If you do, I want to help you be cured! The other option for candidates is to "accept the process" (a saying that I hear more and more commonly adopted in doctoral programs) and put 90% of the work into the prewriting phases so that the laborious final writing phase only takes about 10% of the energy. As I said earlier in this volume, little things add up to big things. If you've ever paid $5 for a cup of coffee every day of the month and received your credit card bill, you can attest to this notion! If you have ever accomplished something like losing body mass toward a healthier weight, lowered your unhealthy blood pressure, or learned how to de-stress through meditation, you know what I am talking about. Small changes — minute, incremental adjustments to your daily work — can over time create huge gains — as some exercise commercials state, "In only 15 minutes a day."

In the last handful of chapters, I've illustrated a framework that you can employ to conduct your review of the literature. I presented you with the five-sources-times-five-quotes model, equaling, at minimum, 25 gathered quotes of progress within a single sitting. I presented you with the matrix that you can use to collect these quotes. I presented you with the four-box method for managing your reading workflow. Now, my request for you is this: Repeat the utilization of these methods, especially the five-times-five method, for 20 weeks. If you employ this framework, gathering 25 quotes a week for 20 weeks, evenly spread across the three, four, or five theory areas that your study touches, you'll have the near-makings of a fully conducted literature review. This assumes a few things:

1. You've adequately gathered quotes across the appropriate historical time periods worth studying. Most people will give a small percentage of their reading time to antiquity (the distant past), a larger percentage of time to each succeeding decade since World War II, and the bulk of their time to those readings that have emerged since 2001.

2. You've gathered quotes from peer-reviewed resources, particularly journal articles, to build the most fundamental building blocks of your logic leading to your study's purpose from those sources emerging since 2001 — and largely in the most recent seven years. Further, you've focused on looking at how questions of a time period led to specific answers discovered, which led to new questions.

3. When you sort your matrix by theory area, sub-theory area, and year, you can see patterns emerging between the authors. Some agree with one another. Others don't agree. You see degrees of agreement emerging.

4. Not necessarily a reliable measure, as your individual situation may differ by your school or program, you should have about 125-150 quotes gathered per theory area, assuming all the items above. In total, you could

easily have 400-500 quotes gathered before proceeding to the post-gathering phase of your literature review. These quotes are spread across dissertations, books, and journal articles (in all their forms). However, many of your quotes will come from journal articles.

With all of your quotes in hand, you are now ready to start the examination of what you have gathered to understand the unfolding story that the literature will offer you.

The most useful aspect of this way of gathering quotes is that you can measure your progress. If you choose to use page count as your way of tracking your progress, this will only be as reliable as the quality of your writing, your understanding of doctoral writing requirements, and your fidelity to what the literature actually says. You *could* write a page of text, and it could be wholly rejected by your dissertation advisor. You *could* write five pages, and all of them could be complete nonsense. However, quotes are clean. As long as you typed one quote worth typing, in its original form, into your matrix, you made one quote's worth of progress. Today, you may only have five quotes in your matrix. Tomorrow, you may have 10, 15, or 20 in your matrix. You could ask your dissertating friend how she is progressing, and she may say, "I've written 20 pages," and you could say in reply, "I've gathered 100 quotes from great sources." Who is guaranteed to be making more progress here? Focus daily on creating small, incremental gains in your quote database until you hit that critical mass of quotes, where you feel like you've covered "it all"! A big matrix is on its way; you are going to build it.

40

SHRED IT

Disclaimer: Not everyone who reads this book will do what I am about to show you. In fact, the contents of this chapter may scare you. If you do what I am about to ask you to consider doing, your spouse may fear you, your children may question your sanity, and anyone with a camera on his or her phone could potentially post unflattering photos of you online. However, with all that said, what I'm about to show you works *so well* in helping you synthesize, organize, and outline your literature review that I think that everyone should at least try it. With all this said, and all this hype created, I want to show you my literature review "shredding" method.

The goal of the literature-review shred is to create a viable outline of your literature review that is in its near-final state of revision from the first attempt. This goal comes with two big caveats: First, remember that nothing is or should be beyond revision; you will revise! However, this method will help you get pretty close! Second, remember that this method is contingent on your completion of all that I have described in this text to the highest degree of academic rigor. Lazy quotes do not produce great outlines. The shred has six steps.

Step 1: Sort Your Matrix. First, using Microsoft® Excel's sorting method, select the entire the document and sort by theory area, sub-theory area, date, and citation. (Note: If you did not utilize Microsoft® Excel to gather your quotes, you'll need to export your quotations to a file readable by this software.) What results from this sort is a chronological list of all your quotes by theory and sub-theory area. Cool!

Step 2: Audit Your Matrix. Even if you have the number of quotes you think you'll need to adequately create an outline of your literature review, you still may be missing huge pieces of the story of each of your theory and sub-theory areas. Remember, the number of quotes is a good measure of progress but not necessarily a measure of "finishedness." Look at each of your sub-theory areas. Do you see any major holes in the years of your quotes? For example, do you see your quotes from 2000, 2001, and 2003 suddenly followed by 2015, 2016, and 2017? What happened to the years 2004-2014? Next, look at the names that appear throughout each of the sub-theory areas. Do you see certain names represented throughout? Do you see some names taking up too much real estate in your matrix compared to others? Is this because these authors are such a big deal, or is it because you did not adequately seek out the writings of others? Do you see certain ideas that everyone agrees on? Is there a lack of counter-notions within a sub-theory area? Is this truly reflective of this sub-theory area? Are more quotes needed from other voices? Repeat this audit for all sub-theory areas. Then, look at the larger main theory areas as a whole, asking these questions. This is the time, the best time, to stop and go back and find more quotes to fill in holes that you see in your information. It will take 10 times the amount of work to add them later if you progress to the next step. Use caution.

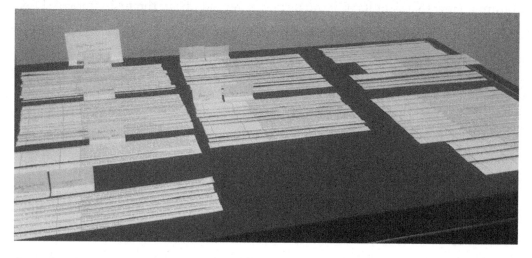

Creating headings and subheadings: a visual literature review

Step 3: Print It. Again, select the entire document. Use Microsoft® Excel's border feature to add internal and external borders to all cells. Essentially, you should be able to print the entire document in such a way that it will look like it has wireframes between all the boxes. Next, select all cells and format them such that "word wrap" is turned on. This will allow you to shorten the length of certain columns such that your document will be one page wide only. Next, work with a tech-savvy friend or tutor to help you adjust your print margins and column widths such that your document will print one page wide (in landscape mode) and X number of pages long. During this step, you'll need to adjust the width of your columns. You'll also need to tell Microsoft® Excel to only print one page wide in landscape. If you have difficulty here, seriously, reach out to someone who can help. It's worth it! Lastly, using a decent-quality paper, print out the entire matrix. Easily, you'll have 40-60 pages worth of printed materials.

Step 4: Shred It. Go to an office supply store and ask for a paper-cutter — the kind that has a straight edge that can cut a strip of paper off of a larger piece of paper. Also, grab a box of big one-gallon or three-gallon zipper bags. Take all your printed pages and shred them across so that each quote is its own strip of paper. Since your pages were already pre-sorted, you'll find it easy to put each set of strips for each theory area into a separate zipper bag. Repeat this until you've shredded your whole matrix.

Step 5: Organize Your Quotes. Now, grab a bag for one of your theory areas. On a table top (with no fans or vents blowing) organize your strips into a progression of logic, leading through each of your sub-theory areas by chronology. Put like ideas next to one another. Put disagreements next to one another. Here, you are only trying to group like ideas. If three authors say the same thing, put those next to one another. If another author says something totally different, look at the date and decide if it goes before or after what each person has said.

Organizing quotes into like ideas

Most quotes organized and "taped"

Step 6: Tape It. Once you have decided on an order of ideas for a specific theory area and all of its sub-theory areas, it's time to commit by placing a piece of tape across a page's worth of quotes. Tape them on a page. Once all pages are done, number the bottom corner of each page to maintain their order. Then, make a clean photocopy of your pages.

WINNING IN YOUR METHODOLOGY CHAPTER

In this section, I'll show you how to connect all the clues better

than a hat-wearing movie archeologist.

41

THE METHOD NORM TRAP

When I was a doctoral candidate, I was not required to take a substantive course in research methods. We talked about academic writing, how to paraphrase and quote sources, and statistics. Never — or, rather, not to my memory — did we discuss the intense differences between qualitative and quantitative research, their aims, and the various ways by which one could go about conducting such research. I wanted to do quantitative work because I did not want to "take the time to interview people." Similarly, I've heard many people *avoiding* quantitative work because they are not, in their words, "a numbers person." Once I started working closely with my own dissertation advisor, I was surprised to learn that there were many different types of quantitative studies and, on the qualitative side, many other brands of methodologies altogether that I could have chosen. Even more surprising was that there were books written on these subjects — guides that I could read. Looking even deeper, I learned that there were authors who had written about the science of research in a step-by-step fashion alongside others who had explored the artful side of research as well. It was not until I started reading these books that I even considered that a study could be "beautiful" or a way by which "truth" could be explored. Long story short, it's possible that a doctoral program may not prepare a dissertation writer for knowing what methodology options are out there, which are most appropriate or most called for by the literature, and the precise steps by which to conduct a selected type of study. In absence of knowledge of these norms, doctoral candidates often fall into what I call the Method Norm

Trap, a pitfall that can cost months and years of heartache.

Doctoral candidates fall into the Method Norm Trap when they blaze forth in writing their introduction, literature review, and methodology chapters without an absolutely firm grasp of (1) what methodology is most appropriate and most called for by the literature and (2) what precise steps they will need to take to collect their data and then analyze it. Speak to the average doctoral candidate in your program who says he or she is "doing a case study." Ask this person what that means. Replies often may come in the form of "interviews!" Others may say, "I'm going to look at one place." Follow-up questions from there to such a person may, in your doctoral program's culture, feel impolite. Here are the big questions that often will appear in your proposal defense and final oral defense:

1. Of all the methodologies out there, why did you select this one?

2. What other researchers, and what voices in the literature, have called for the methodology you have selected?

3. Give the long answer: What does it mean to do a [blank] study?

4. Again, the long answer: What are the precise 10-30 steps you will take to collect this data?

5. Even longer answer: What are the precise data analysis steps that you will take?

The cure for these questions is good answers, and good answers come from listening to the literature (having the attention and patience to listen) and steeping yourself in the norms of the methodology that you have selected. These norms, the accepted ways by which your type of study is conducted and how your methodology can and should be used within research, arise from three distinct voices that you will need to explore prior to attempting to float your study idea to your chair, before you write much of anything, and before you attempt to conduct the study.

Methodology Norm 1: The Experts. There are researchers, practitioners, and simply impressive human beings like Creswell, Stake, Yin, Charmaz, and many others who have spent their careers and writing time speaking to the art and science of specific research methodologies. Considering their efforts, it behooves you to inquire about their texts, read them, and live them as a scholar practitioner. Creswell's (2006) seminal text, *Qualitative Inquiry and Research Design: Choosing Among Five Approaches*, is my favorite qualitative text, one that I am constantly recommending to doctoral candidates who are considering qualitative research. Books put out by these authors provide the ultimate specifics regarding WHY one would utilize such a methodology (because each methodology accomplishes different things) and EXACTLY HOW one would go about (1) collecting and (2) analyzing the data. You can find an expansive list of books that I recommend, broken down by methodology, on my website.

www.TheDissertationMentor.com

Methodology Norm 2: The Literature. Just as the selection of your methodology needs to be supported by the literature, typically meaning that other researchers are calling for you to do such a study, the work of other researchers provides clear clues about what it looks like to conduct such a study. Not all that you see will be true to form, though! I've seen case studies wearing phenomenological clothing. I've seen ethnographies disguised as case studies. I've seen bad math hocus pocus. Be careful! But do pay attention to what is being done by others.

Methodology Norm 3: Your Program. Believe it or not, your doctoral program, and the norms of research within it, can have a huge impact on how your study will be conducted — for right or for wrong. Look at the hard work of other students who came before you. See how they went about undertaking your methodology of choice. Keep in mind, though, that at this level, biases abound. Just because you see it being done does not mean it's right. Even we professors get it wrong occasionally.

42

THE INSTRUMENTATION TRAP

Some doctoral candidates are best served by utilizing the data collection protocols of others (with citation and credit, of course). Specifically, when it comes to surveys administered, interviews given, and observations conducted, it can be useful to look at what others have done before and ask yourself, "To what degree do I need to reinvent this?" Often, especially in the humanities and social sciences, candidates who want to conduct interviews end up inventing a series of questions that they feel are important to ask, revising those questions slightly through their review of the literature, and then attempting to "fly it" to their dissertation advisor to see if their protocol passes muster. Just as often, such candidates are disappointed that they are asked to revise the questions and provide justification for the questions being asked. Even worse is when candidates invent a complicated assessment to measure leadership acuity, coaching ability, or "the impact" of XYZ, only to find that they are challenged on the importance of such questions, the reliability and validity of their instrument, and its deep components of construction. Entire texts, dozens and dozens of them, are dedicated to how to build survey instruments, interview protocols, and standardized assessments. Doctoral candidates find themselves with questions to consider in this regard:

1. Do I subject myself to the time, growth, and patience to develop my own instrument or assessment?

2. Does my research design truly require me to build something from scratch or something so complicated as what I am attempting to utilize?

3. Given my deepening understanding I am developing (because I am reading books by the experts and looking at the norms within the literature and my program), what type of survey, instrument, or assessment is most appropriate?

4. Should I adopt the survey, instrument, assessment, or protocol developed by someone else?

Ultimately, great research is very, *very* specific in its aims, and great researchers are exceedingly careful about how they go about what they are attempting. So, is it possible that you may be overcomplicating things with your 100-question survey?

There are also your participants, if you have them and they are human, to consider. Would they take the time of their own free will to subject themselves to your survey, instrument, assessment, or protocol? How much time is required of them to do so? If they are getting it in the mail, via email, or via link, and you are not present to awkwardly stare at them until they finish it or to apply sufficient peer pressure (if they even know you), will they have any likely reason to complete it? Adding up all the time that all of your participants would have to take to complete *your survey*, does that number seem a bit unlikely to you? Time your instrument. If it takes 10 minutes to complete and you need 100 participants, that's 1,000 minutes (over 16 hours) of manpower required. Consider: When was the last time you filled out some random survey that hit your inbox? In the busyness of your day, if you heard that some stranger was down the hall conducting interviews for research and that 20 minutes of your precious time would be required to volunteer for the thing, would *even you* take the time to volunteer? When humans are involved, you have to consider *why anyone* like your participants would take the time to help you out.

Finally, there is a financial cost to consider. If you are using a copyrighted instrument, survey, or assessment, you'll need to get permission to utilize it. If you don't know if it's copyrighted, assume that it is and believe that you'll probably have to get the blessing of someone to utilize it. Often, especially in the case of assessments, this requires a financial payment. Sometimes, instruments come in "packs" of 10, meaning you may have to pay for two packs to survey 11-20 people. Sometimes, you'll have to direct people to a specific website with a specific payment or participant code. Sometimes, you'll be able to make copies of the instrument yourself, other times not. Some instruments won't even be touched by you, as they will be sent on your behalf to a list of email or physical addresses you provide! If you are using SurveyMonkey.com, you might have to pay a fee. If you are sending unsolicited emails, there are SPAM laws to consider. The list goes on and on.

To avoid the pitfalls of the Instrumentation Trap, a conundrum that can freeze you in place for months and years, think about the *most essential* questions (or question) that your study is attempting to answer. What is the cleanest route to exploring that question or those questions? If you kept chipping away at the marble block of all that you have read and all that you have attempted to write, what *really* is being examined here? Could it be that someone else has already found a way to understand, capture, or typograph this in one of the most clean, acceptable ways known to date? Always, I would prefer that a candidate have a short, well-written, specific survey, interview protocol, or assessment rather than a verbose collection of what the candidate thinks "should be asked" of his or her participants. Just as you did with the Method Norm Trap, look at the great work of others. How did they approach what you are approaching in your study? Accordingly, what's the best course of action to take next?

43

SCRIPT IT

In a matter of weeks or months (with a great deal of hard work), your editor, your methodologist, your institutional review board (IRB), your advisor, and your committee will have a chance to see your full proposal draft, your initial chapters, for the first time. Among many matters that will be on their minds, these individuals will be wondering about the absolutely defined, precise steps that you will be taking to collect and analyze your data. It's not enough to say that you are doing a quantitative descriptive, correlational study or quasi-experimental study; you need to be prepared (as I've discussed in the previous chapters) to define what that means, why it's appropriate given the previous research that's been conducted, and why it's the appropriate research approach for what you are attempting to understand. Even more important is your ability to soberly discuss the individual steps that you will take to collect and analyze the data that you so anxiously want to get into your hands.

For my purposes with you here in this text, I want you to know these steps so you know precisely what you are getting yourself into. I recall one student with whom I was consulting; she worked in a large metropolitan school district on the West Coast of the United States and wanted to utilize students within her school district for the purposes of data collection. She discovered that to do so would require an authorization to utilize the premises by the school board, which would take months to obtain. She learned that she would also have to do an "internal IRB" application in her organization, which would take up to a year to complete.

Further, on top of all of that, she would have to provide translators for the approximately 24 languages represented at the school sites she intended to utilize for her study, to ensure that parents understood what they were signing when they approved their students' participation in this study. For her situation, learning about the individual steps of her study was a lifesaver. For her specific situation, there was so much involved with this course of study that she decided on another topic altogether. Another client of mine was surprised to learn that certain statistical tests require a minimum number of data points (or participants). This client could not run the statistical tests of significance that she wanted to run unless she found 50 more people to be part of her study. So, discovering and listing out the steps of your data collection and data analysis is not simply a matter of meeting the requirements of your chair; it's part of the process of ensuring the feasibility of your study — the "doability" of the whole endeavor. It's a chance for you (as you'll see in the following chapter) to examine when you could, potentially, defend and graduate.

On another note, listing the steps of your study can give your participants (if you have any) the absolute justice that they deserve in being your participants. You will have people pouring out their lives to you, parading out their skeletons with a great deal of trust; I truly hope you've earned their trust in the work you've put into ensuring that their voices are heard accurately through your survey, assessment, interview, observation, and so on. You may even be working with people who are facing significant challenges in life. I've worked with students who were studying the mentally ill, the homeless, minors, the incarcerated, and the elderly. There are not only legal concerns when working with individuals such as these but also significant ethical concerns. In the most basic sense, I want you to understand that you owe a great debt to those who participate in your study. When working with human beings, you are becoming a sacred holder of their stories. Accordingly, you owe it to them to present what they give you in the most accurate and sound way possible. You have to create a plan worthy of their contributions. I want you to be able to look at your dissertation years from now and know that everything that is in there is accurate, appropriate, and ultimately justice-giving.

Here is the process for listing out your steps of data collection and analysis. First, engage in the considerations listed in the previous chapters. Obtain books wherein experts detail the steps of applying the approach that you have selected. Get copies of studies, including dissertations from your program, that employed your methodology. Second, looking at all of these documents, list out the various steps taken in each study to obtain and collect data. Consider creating a matrix where you list, across the columns, the various studies and, down the rows, the many steps they took. Ultimately, give the greatest weight to a healthy, robust hybrid of the experts' named steps and your program's typical execution of those steps as seen in its dissertations. In a separate document, create a list of those hybrid steps. Provide citations in your numbered list of steps for the sources where you found each of the steps. Third, locate another book or two from experts in the methodology you have selected. Look at the steps that they name. What steps are similar? Add citations appropriately and expand your list of steps. Fourth, as if you were only once more going to review and adapt this list to your own study, go through each individual step and add the various specific steps that may have been overlooked, such as the phone script that you will use to contact others, the method of obtaining contact information for your participants, the precise script you will utilize when conducting your interviews (including the precise forms that you will use when obtaining informed consent and giving notice of confidentiality, and even when you will hit the "record" button). Finally, repeat the same process for your data analysis, paying special attention to those moments in examining the statistical steps when you are tempted to ignore or bypass an item you don't understand. Understand every step.

MAY
S M T W T F S
1 2 3 4 5 6
7 8 9 10 11 12 13
14 15 16 17 18 19 20
21 22 23 24 25 26 27
28 29 30 31
GRADUATION DAY!

44

TIMELINE

In my doctoral program, students were responsible for finding their own dissertation chairs. We were humorously invited to "date" our chairs by meeting with them in person or calling them on the phone and interviewing them to see if we were a good fit for one another. We were allowed to take this step of finding a chair once we had adequately completed a number of classes and were able to produce an initial, very rough draft of our introductory chapter of our dissertation. The same week that I "advanced" to be able to reach out to potential chairs, I had three calls scheduled with three faculty members within my program. The first two of these calls went very much the same. Most importantly, as I was about 18 months from finishing my official coursework, I inquired about how long it could take to finish my dissertation. Both of these first two faculty members said that I could finish as quickly as I wanted if I put my mind to it and made changes in my life to make that happen. However, when I spoke to the third potential chair, I got a much different reply to this question. When I asked if she believed it would be possible to finish, she, very directly, stated something to the effect of, "Guy, you will be hard-pressed to even have your data collected within the next 18 months. It could easily take you two or more years to finish, even if you work very, *very* hard." Feeling a bit numb in the face, I asked if she would explain that to me – and she did. She spent the next 45 minutes on the phone with me, walking me through each of the steps of my dissertation and having me hypothesize how long each step might take. Needless to say, not only did she become my chair, but her statements proved accurate, and my hypotheses about the various stages of my dissertation timeline came true.

When you are honest with yourself about your timeline, when you know the work ahead of you, you are far more likely, in my experience, to be able to take up the cause of finishing this dissertation. If you know the road is two years long, you are more able to be ready for that journey. However, if you think you are only months away but your work ends up proving to take many more months or years, you might just stop working altogether. So many candidates have ended up working with me after *years* of doing nothing in their dissertation work. I want you to be fully aware of what is coming. My chair revealed to me a clear picture of what would be required of me to finish. Isn't that what you want too?

The dissertation process is a recursive process involving moving forward, revising, moving a bit more forward, and revising, with many required engagements and interactions with formal processes within your university. Even if you write the perfect dissertation, you cannot bypass the formal processes AND THE TIME CONSTRAINTS IMPOSED by your university. If the university's ethics (IRB) process takes months to resolve, that is not something you can bypass. If the institution has a quality review apparatus that examines your work after your chair has approved it, you still must wait. What my chair did for me was explain to me, in quite simple terms, why graduating within the next school year (in my personal situation) was not feasible. Accordingly, this chapter's activity, in an ultimately detailed fashion, will lay out a fairly precise schedule that you will need to follow to best meet your intended graduation date.

Consulting your university, advisor, and dissertation handbook (often provided by your program at your university), complete the following timeline activity. Start with your target graduation date, utilizing the actual date of the graduation, if possible. Then, backward map your schedule based on the questions asked. In the end, you may discover that your timeline is not properly scaled for your personal situation. For example, you may realize that you cannot plausibly graduate within the timeline expected. If this is the case, make the necessary adjustments to the timeline so that it works for you. Finally, once you have a timeline that is feasible (though it may be quite ambitious), place it in your calendar. If you use a digital calendar, set reminders 45, 30, and 15 days away from each of the benchmarks identified. The following assumes a five-chapter dissertation:

19. When is my target graduation date?

18. When is the last day to submit final revisions to my university's quality review apparatus or "library reader" after defense?

17. When is the last day to submit final revisions to my committee after defense?

16. When is the last day to defend?

15. When is the last day to submit my final defense form?

14. When will Chapters 4-5 be committee approved?

13. When will Chapters 4-5 be approved by my chair?

12. When will Chapters 4-5 be approved by my editor*?

11. When will I be done writing Chapters 4-5?

10. When will my statistical analysis be complete?

9. When will I be done collecting my data?

8. When will I request data from my participants?

7. When will I be ready to send requests to potential participants or the organizations that represent them?

6. When will my university's IRB approve my study?

5. When will my university's quality review apparatus approve my introduction, literature review, and methodology chapters?

4. When will my committee approve these chapters?

3. When will my chair approve these chapters?

2. When will my editor* and I be able to complete final revisions
    on these chapters?

1. When will I be done writing my near-final draft of my introduction,
    literature review, and methodology chapters?

*Note: Editors are not allowed by some schools. Sometimes, only "editing coaches" are permitted. Consult your academic or dissertation advisor at your school regarding this. See my examination of this topic in Chapter 10.

SOME WRITING ADVICE

In this section, I have you take a good look in the mirror.

45

WHAT'S MY EMAIL ADDRESS?

Here it is: guy@thedissertationmentor.com

Yes. That is really my email address.

If you email me there, I will read your email. However, I can't guarantee that I'll reply. Here's how you can improve the chance of getting me to reply to your email, if that is something that interests you:

1. Send me a specific question. I love when questions are specific.

2. Tell me who you are! I want to know about your university, your program, the professors there who have rocked your world. I want to hear about your dreams and aspirations that are drawing you to complete a doctoral degree.

3. Tell me your biggest challenges. Tell me the things that keep you up at night, stress you out, or cause you any bit of anxiety related to your dissertation.

4. Tell me about any books or videos that have been helpful to you. What podcasts do you listen to? Do you follow any experts or voices in your area of study?

5. Please don't ask me to review your dissertation, attaching a file, saying how grateful you'd be if I'd review the 200-page document and provide comment as a favor. (Seriously, I get about five of these review requests a week.)

Still, if you don't want to take the chance of not getting a reply, you can turn to social media.

If you post a picture of yourself with the cover of this book on my Facebook® page (www.facebook.com/TheDissertationMentor) and ask a clear, specific question, I will nearly always respond. Though I can't make a guarantee here, you're probably about 99.9% likely to have your question answered if you slap your selfie with this book into my social media world — because when I reply to you, I get to answer your question for thousands and thousands of people to see. In many circumstances, I will be moved to produce a video about your question if I've not before covered it in my show, *Office Hours with Dr. Guy*.

Do me one favor though, please: Email me and tell me what you think of this book so far. Tell me what I could be doing better. Tell me where I "nailed it." Tell me how I can help you. I will always do my best to help you out of your writing conundrum.

46

THE EVIL "I"

Every writer in academia has heard a professor say, "Leave the 'I' out of it! Don't write 'I' in your paper!" Since a young age, this has always struck me as strange. In the vast majority of doctoral programs, dissertations are not personal documents; they are not reflective in any manner. They are about the research, the process of your study, and the results and conclusions that came out of it. As I've heard it said many times in many classrooms at this level, "You don't get to show up in your dissertation until the last chapter." Still, as I made a strong case for at the start of this book, there are few endeavors that you will undertake that are more *personal* than your doctoral study and the dissertation that results from it. Further, since my youth, I've always been of the opinion that all writing, especially that which will be published, is deeply personal, deeply important work that we cannot divorce from the author. After all, regardless of how little you show up in this dissertation, *you* will be there in those lines of text long after your body has left the planet. Far enough down the line, this dissertation may be the only thing left of "you" on this planet at all! To me, this makes your work in your dissertation deeply personal. Still, academic writing, at least in this and the last handful of epochs of human history, tends toward holding the "I" at bay. In this quick chapter, I want to tell you where you can (perhaps not so subtly) sneak yourself into your dissertation project.

First, write a one-line or so dedication page. If you are like most people, this will be the first place your words will appear in published print anywhere. When one learns how to program, the default code that is typed in the first project nearly always outputs "Hello World" onto the screen. What do you want to be your "hello world" when people open up this thing for the first time? Often, I find it best for candidates to consider the larger, world-altering, deeply meaningful purpose that is drawing them through a doctoral program. Think about the people you want to help through your finishing of your doctorate; consider dedicating your dissertation to them!

Second, it's time to write a two- to five-page love note: Write your acknowledgement pages. Thank everyone by name who has helped you or allowed you to finish this dissertation (or, at least, get this far in the process). People to consider are your dissertation chair, your committee members, important faculty members, staff supports at your school, mentors, confidants, peers in arms, your spouse, your children, your parents, your boss, authors (like those I mentioned earlier in this book), and even seminal thinkers, philosophers, and scientists in your field. If you've ever watched an award show and thought, "Wow, I hope she remembers to thank all those people who got her there on that stage," this is your moment within your dissertation that could be your last chance, your final word to ensure that everyone who deserves those words of thanks gets his or her name in black text on paper or PDF. Later on, this list of persons can also function as a list that you'll use for party invites, thank-you notes, and gift planning. Further, this is the place where you get to insert a bit about your life, what led you to your doctoral work, and the stage of your life at this moment.

Third, create an appendix in your dissertation called "About the Author." Insert a photo of yourself along with a three-paragraph biography about yourself as if this were going to appear on a website for your consulting services relating to your dissertation topic. Spend the first sentence saying who you are and what you do. Spend the rest of the first paragraph talking about what kind of services you offer as a consultant in your field. If you don't offer these yet, imagine that you do and write it anyway. Spend the second paragraph talking about your experience and expertise. In the third paragraph, talk about the key questions that you will explore with your clients when you begin working together. Conclude by including your contact information. Let this be the marketing template for, potentially, the next phase of your life as a doctoral person. What if your program won't allow this? Wait for someone to ask you to delete it. If someone from your program asks you to remove it, then remove it.

Finally, when you are done with your study, create another appendix that converts your entire dissertation into a two-page flyer, as if it were a one-sheet report, brief executive summary, or small journal article. Divide the flyer into the same number of chapters as your dissertation. In a single paragraph in each section, give the briefest possible summary of each chapter. You'll probably have (1) introduction, (2) literature review, (3) methodology, (4) findings, and (5) conclusions sections. Now, spend time beefing up the findings and conclusions sections of this summary. Specifically highlight those items that you feel are most important for recommendations for research and practice for practitioners in your field. Make this thing as valuable as they come — something that you would covet at a conference and, perhaps, even pay to receive. Imagine that your boss's boss would never read a 200- to 300-page dissertation, but she may read your two-page summary — or at least the last five bullet points where you lay out the next big thing at your place of work! As I tell my candidates, always be feathering your future nest. Soon, the results of your accomplishment may be on the desks of some very important people. You'll have only a few seconds of their attention. You need to have your materials ready for such a moment.

47

DEVELOP YOUR SCHOLARLY VOICE

I just told you a bunch of places where you get to show up in your dissertation. Here are places you can't show up: everywhere else — at least as an "I" speaking person, or even as "the researcher." As an academic writer, you are developing your voice of scholarship. It's like learning to speak another language; you should be encouraged to practice speaking this language throughout your earlier coursework leading you to your dissertation writing phase. Early on, you are going to make some serious errors in your speaking and writing in your developing scholarly voice. However, by the end of the journey, you will be able to sit within a room of knowledgeable muckety-mucks, your new peers in scholarship (your dissertation committee), and present using this language. In these final moments of your dissertation path, assuming that you defend successfully, you will fully embody the scholar — one who thinks, writes, and speaks as a scholar — and you'll keep growing as a scholar as you advance in life. As I'm writing about this a bit here, it strikes me that there are entire texts out there about this topic — ones that I hope you are encouraged to read by your doctoral program. In light of this, let me spend some time today defining scholarly voice for you and talking about the top ways you can work to develop this voice.

Your "scholarly voice" is your ultimate, informed, bias-free, incredibly precise language — well-versed presentation without fallacy or hyperbole. You don't have to tell your readers that something is "important," "crucial," or "critical" because you are showing them the magnitude of your statements that are backed up by the literature: Other scholars are saying "this" (whatever this is), not just you! Further, it's not that the scholars even agree with you at all; scholars present the whole picture — those who agree with the central line of logic and those who don't. As you develop in this way of speaking and writing, you'll be able to have conversations at a logically sound, high level. You'll be able to say that a group of researchers, theorists, and practitioners see things one way while a whole other group sees things another way, and you'll also be able to discuss the degrees of agreement between these groups. As I've said, developing this voice takes a great deal of practice. Here are a few ways that I want you to practice this during your writing and speaking sessions.

First, look at any paragraph in your dissertation draft and evaluate the scholarly voice. How many sentences in this paragraph have citations? Take a highlighter and highlight all those sentences that have citations attached to them. Next, look for all the sentences that you would consider common knowledge — those statements that any and all reasonable persons would agree are true without controversy. Look at such sentences again with *great* skepticism. Are there assumptions that you are making about the widespread acceptance of these "common knowledge" sentences? Are these sentences colloquialisms? Hyperbole? If you still feel that these sentences are, indeed, common knowledge without disagreement, highlight them too. Now, look at those sentences in the paragraph that are not highlighted; they bare no citations and are not common knowledge. So, where did they come from? Chances are, they are from *you* — your opinion, your views, your assumptions about the subject matter about which you are speaking. You are showing up in your writing in a big way — and you're not allowed to do that and call it scholarly voice. Make the language of such sentences exceedingly precise, add citations for the work of those scholars who agree with what is being said, or remove the sentences altogether.

Second, examine a paragraph for its quality of critical analysis. Are alternative views, besides the one that you are presenting, presented? To what degree do you define the main logical point of the paragraph in the first sentence? To what degree do you use the sentences that follow to describe what you stated at the start of the paragraph? To what degree do you provide specific examples from the literature to support what you are stating? Even more important for doctoral-level writing, to what degree do you compare and contrast (examine the similarities and differences of) *various* scholars within your paragraph? Do you show the degree of agreement between them? Ultimately, what conclusions can your readers draw from the summary of all that you have presented in this paragraph? Further, look at the main point of the paragraph before this and the paragraph that follows. To what degree does this paragraph create a building block of the growing logic of your discussion, leading to the climax of your chapter? Do you tell the story of a viewpoint? Or, alternatively and less impressively, do you only show one side of the story?

Finally, examine the level of synthesis that is present within your writing. Synthesis could be defined as the distilling of many into one. Within your paragraphs, your readers should see that you did not glean a piece of your logical sequence (a sentence, for example) simply from one source; they should see evidence that you drew from many sources. So, what percentage of your sentences have more than one citation attached (e.g., "Peter, 2012; Talus, 2014; Zenith, 2017")? Would you say that few of your sentences show this level of synthesis? Do your paragraphs begin with one-off citations like "Smith (2009) found that..." and so on? Focus on telling the story from all of the sources you accessed during your review of the literature.

DISSERTATION CHAIRS, COMMITTEE MEMBERS, AND GETTING ACROSS THE FINISH LINE

In this section, I talk about finishing well.

48

CRITIQUE IT

In your final chapter of your dissertation, and in the oral defense that will shortly follow, you will be using a type of scholarly voice that is worth discussing. Think about your first days on the job. For me, I was a brand-new teacher suddenly responsible for the safety, well-being, and reading and writing levels of 150 supposedly "remedial" high school students. I was 24 years old, had just quit my position as a restaurant manager, and thought that I knew what being a teacher was going to be all about. I assigned more homework in a week than these students had ever received during an entire semester before, I held tight to slightly-insane deadlines, and I wrote six detentions in the first day. It took me about five days to realize that I knew *nothing* about the actual experience of teaching inside of a classroom. Nowadays, when I'm put in front of a group of educators, as I've had *much* experience teaching teenagers, I can absolutely showcase my knowledge and expertise. If you paired me up with a brand-new teacher, I could teach that person a thing or two about teaching! Similarly, because of your experience on the job, I have no doubt that you could teach a brand-new person in your field much about what to expect, what he or she may encounter, and how to meet the challenges that he or she will surely face. With your experiences grows expertise, and your expertise allows you to speak, write, and teach as one who has such a high level of understanding. Your dissertation is exactly like this: The more you know, the more you have studied, the more you have synthesized all that you have read into your draft, and the more you build great logic, the more you will be able to speak from that level of critical expertise *only* possible in a candidate who is prepared to write his or her final chapter and to defend his or her dissertation.

As you pivot from writing your introductory chapters to collecting and analyzing your data, to finally making some conclusions about what you found and presenting that to your committee at oral defense, there is a style of writing that I want to present to you. It's not enough to simply tell them what you found. After all, you probably *found* lots of things! You have to decide what are the "key findings" among all that you could draw forth from the data that is now in your hands. If you have not yet conducted your review of the literature, it will be very difficult to complete this step, as it's the knowledge, understanding, and expertise that you garnered from your review of the literature that you need to draw from when you are in the final stages of your writing. When looking at your findings and interpreting them, consider what you saw in the literature. What did you expect to find, given all that the literature said? To what degree did you expect to find this? As you look at your data and analyze, you'll see that what you found confirmed, refuted, or advanced the literature. That is, your data could have confirmed what the literature said was probably going to happen. Your data may have refuted what the literature said (what often prompts me to say, "Hmmm…innnnnteresting!"). Also, the data could have advanced (not only confirmed but *extra*-confirmed) the literature. Once you have a grasp of what your data is showing you and how it relates to what the literature would have anticipated, you get to make some judgments about the key findings that you name. You'll always show *all* of your findings, but it's expected that you highlight those findings that are most worthy of presentation. In your findings chapter (or chapters), for example, you may divide your presentation of the data by research question. You could also choose to organize your presentation by the various themes that emerged through your analysis. Regardless, I recommend presenting the key findings in summary somewhere.

Your final chapter of your dissertation is where your critical, scholarly voice will make one final appearance before oral defense. Here, you'll do a five-step dance that will tie everything together. Here are the steps of that dance that you'll repeat for each of your key findings:

1. First, present the key finding in a sentence or two or three. What did you find through the course of your study?

2. Second, discuss what the literature said *beforehand* regarding the subject of this finding. Paint a picture of what ground researchers laid before you in terms of this finding. What would you have expected?

3. Third, make it clear how this key finding relates to the information that was presented in the literature. Does this finding confirm, refute, or advance the literature?

4. Fourth, again using the literature, discuss how various scholars do or could make sense of this key finding.

5. Finally, pivot the language in such a way that you walk as close as possible to making a recommendation for research or a recommendation for practice without actually making it. Instead, make a note to yourself regarding such recommendations and place them later in the chapter in the appropriate section.

For the purpose of practicing for oral defense, spend time awkwardly in your car or office, alone, speaking to yourself in this five-step dance. Practice repeating these five steps orally as a way to take in the relationship between what you found in the literature, what you found through the data, how others might make sense of that, and what you recommend accordingly.

49

YOU, THE EXPERT

Soon, there will come a day when you will be sitting at a table with (or looking at) your advisor and your committee members to defend your dissertation. It's possible that you'll have your peers, other faculty members, and family present for this meeting. The oral defense, contrary to the image that you may have built in your head, is not really a do-or-die question-and-answer interrogation. Instead, it's a presentation followed by a scholarly conversation. At the start of your doctoral coursework, your scholarly voice was brand new. You may have even known about some of the literature and much about what happens in your field in the experience of practitioners. By the end of your doctoral journey, your scholarly voice will be developed to the point where you are able to think, speak, and otherwise operate within your field among others as a scholarly practitioner — one whose words, thinking, and actions are guided by a healthy mix of highly informed engagement and knowledge in the literature alongside strong practice, constantly being refined. If you think about the heroes in most epics, the end of the journey is just the beginning for them. Such heroes in mythology often either return home with new knowledge and tools or transcend the world of their village altogether and go somewhere *else*. The oral defense, and your successful completion of it, marks the last inch that borders between everything that has led to this moment and everything that you will do going forward as your scholarly self. Pause and consider this for a moment. Everything you are doing is leading you to a final trial that consists of a scholarly conversation; after that, anything is possible (more on that later).

You are not sitting in the hot seat of this conversation as a student; you're sitting there as an expert.

If you are reading this chapter as you are pulling the teeth of your early dissertation chapters, before you have collected and analyzed your data or critiqued and evaluated your findings among the constellation of the literature to date, you probably feel like anything *but* an expert. My brothers and sisters in arms who are in these early stages, I want to ask you to push on, keep moving forward, and maintain those daily practices that will allow you to build the knowledge, familiarity, and expertise I discussed earlier in this volume. Think about the type of work that will have to happen each day, the brand of engagement that you'll have to undertake to be able to sit in a room with your advisor, your committee, and, potentially, a number of scholars in your field of study and be able to say, "I'm the expert in this room about this study." That's the goal. Let that sink in. Let that influence your daily work.

Now, for the hardworking few who will end up at oral defense, take the advice that I have seen given to defending candidates by their advisors: Remember that if your advisor has given you the chance to sit in that chair and present and defend your dissertation, you are the expert in the room about your study. Those sitting with you that day are there to learn from your hard work and your expertise. You have spent the months and years burying yourself in the literature of your theory areas. You have spent just as much time engaging with your participants (if you had any) and mining through your data. You met the challenges of the statistical tests and mathematical magicianry required to make sense of all that you collected. You even delved further back into the literature to understand the relationship of your findings to the findings that scholars presented previous to your study. Here, in this meeting, you get to take your seat as the expert. Preparing for this meeting will be like nothing you have done before. You must prepare as the expert, not as the student you have been for so many years.

Preparing for your oral defense takes many forms. As an expert who will soon give *the* presentation of his or her academic life thus far, you need to pick up a few things and put down some others:

1. Pick up the story of your life that led you to a doctoral degree, what you saw in your workplace or field that made you want to focus on this study, and how this story will continue forward after you have completed your doctoral degree. Be ready to weave together the whole story for the ears of your committee.

2. Pick up the habit of talking regularly, repeatedly — even to the chagrin of your spouse, friends, and colleagues — regarding what you found in the literature that led you to this study, the purpose of your study, and the precise steps you took to collect data for your study.

3. Pick up the precise, discerning, focused language that will be required for you to communicate your findings without overstepping into unscholarly hyperbole or speculation. Learn how to communicate just the facts and the exact extent to which the literature could support any further speculation.

4. Ask your peers and coaches to put down the "nice" act. Have them ask you truly brutal, tough questions about your study. Have them purposely attempt to ruffle your nicely groomed feathers. Get messy. Feel what that feels like so that you can take a few hits in the oral defense.

5. Lastly, put down your need to give an answer even if you don't know the answer. Learn to discern and describe what you *can say*, illustrate where you step into an area you don't know about, and talk about sources to which you may turn when you don't know.

50

MAKE IT AN ARRIVAL

Throughout your dissertation writing, whether you are just about to provide your first chapter "prospectus" or concept paper to your chair, submit your proposal draft to your committee, submit your final chapters prior to defense, or even construct the physical environment of your oral defense meeting, it's important that you create the experience of the magnitude of meeting these stages. As I've argued in much of my writing and speaking regarding education, there are few places in our lives where we can satisfy the inborn yearning we have for rites of passage. When I was 12 years old, I entered the Boy Scouts of America through a rite of passage involving a small bridge on a stage in front of a few dozen other boys. The bridge symbolized the crossing from boyhood into manhood. On the boyhood side stood my parents, and on the other side stood my soon-to-be peers in my new "troop." For the preteen me, this was a big deal, and it had profound impacts on the way I saw myself, my interactions with others, and my way of engaging in my work at school. After all, I was, in my own words to my mother, "a man now." Likewise, throughout life, I have used moments such as these ("small crossings," I call them) to mark the episodes of my unfolding journey. Researchers, philosophers, and practitioners alike understand the value of such rites of passage. Sadly, in this culture in which I live, so many of these important life moments go unacknowledged or have been removed completely from our way of life. Simply put, you too need small rites of passage to permeate your work as a dissertation writer. You need the acknowledgement and energy that such rites invoke. Further, your advisor and committee members need you to display the developmental stages of a "finishing" candidate.

With each interaction, you are constantly conditioning your dissertation chair and committee members to make assessments about your preparedness for finishing. It's possible that some of the actions that you are taking in your most seemingly casual interactions are convincing them further that you are not progressing — and that your emails, communications, and interactions are something to be delayed or avoided altogether. I met a candidate last year, for example, who was convinced that her chair was no longer reading her work. Through some conversational digging, the student admitted that she had sent no fewer than 20 rough drafts to her chair within the past two years, rarely fixing those items that the chair requested in his original feedback. Through time, no doubt, the chair came to believe that the candidate already had everything she needed to make the required changes. How many times did he have to give feedback to this candidate for it to stick? On the opposite end of such a spectrum, I've seen candidates who sent a small handful of minor communications to their chairs to gain clarity around certain topics, scheduled phone calls to collaborate and align expectations, and came through with highly polished "near-final" drafts for their chairs. The chairs of such candidates quickly learned that these candidates were not only making progress but were, with each interaction, each email, each round of revisions, and each draft, making substantive progress toward finishing. Accordingly, when the time came for the crossing between one stage of the dissertation writing process and another, the chairs felt, along with the candidates, the gravity of the accomplishment. The great work to which candidates committed was coming to fruition! It's incredibly exciting for a dissertation chair to see his or her candidate make an arrival at a new stage. The most exciting moment is seeing candidates successfully defend, because they have finally arrived at the end of this journey and are ready to step into another.

When you deliver a draft to your chair, recall that Final Draft Pledge (Chapter 20) that I urged you to make earlier in this volume. Don't just send it via email; consider printing out that bad boy, flagging the breaks between chapters, placing it into a FedEx® Overnight box with your chair's favorite candy and a note that reads,

> "Dear Dr. So-and-so,
>
> It's with great excitement that I attach my 'near-final' draft of my proposal. My hope is that you will read this and be able to provide any feedback that will allow me to move forward and start collecting data. I've put in as much work as I can without your feedback. Truly, this is the best work I've ever put into a paper. I humbly look forward to receiving your feedback and suggestions. Thank you for all you are doing in my life, academically and beyond.
>
> With great respect,
> Cathy the Candidate
> Email: email@email.com
> Phone: (XXX) XXX-XXXX"

"Why a FedEx® box?" you might ask. Because who in the world receives a FedEx® box and signs for it without immediately opening it to examine its contents? Make it an arrival!

Overall, I hope you have garnered from this short chapter that the best thing you can do for yourself is to recognize the gravity of completing each stage of your writing, put forth the *best* work possible, and when you truly believe it's as close as possible to final, make it a major moment when you pop that thing in the mail. Then, go out for a celebration with your spouse or friends. Eat cheesy food. Have an expensive beverage. Make a toast to your future.

51

SERVE FOOD

The ultimate arrival for the Dissertation Warrior is the oral defense and its successful outcome. It's the moment when the door to your unlimited future will be in front of you, and all that has led to this moment will stand behind you. It's a powerful moment wherein you get to hold tightly the ribbons of past and present, drawing forth all that you have learned, experienced, and undertaken in the past years to draw you closer to that threshold of finishing. You have the whole of your future in front of you; the options are wide open, the energy will be more plentiful, and your schedule will become anything you want it to be — you're going to be free of this undertaking. Few times in life offer such a moment of sacred in-between. I vividly remember my high school graduation — after receiving my diploma, sitting in the aisles of hundreds of faces that I had seen for years before, knowing that I would probably never see many of these people ever again. I remember watching a dear friend in my life, many years ago, disappear in the rearview mirror of my vehicle after saying goodbye for the last time. I remember seeing my bride in her wedding dress for the first time. I remember seeing my children's faces for the first time. I remember the moment my chair looked me in the eyes in front of the entire room of my most important friends and family and said, "May I be the first to congratulate you, Dr. White." Always be mindful of situations such as these, where there is such a clean split between the eras of your life. We are born, we grow old, we marry, we have children, and we die. There are so few guarantees in this short life; take notice of what you have while you have it as these moments are sacred and precious. Soon, you'll be arriving at one of the most defining moments of your life: the culmination of your doctoral journey.

The oral defense is a Rite of Passage (with capital letters). It marks the moment that you are stepping into the ranks of scholarly practitioners. Should you successfully defend, you will be sitting among your committee members as peers. You'll have shown that you have completed the most rigorous academic challenge that you could undertake, that you are able to engage as a scholar in the world, and that you have fulfilled all of the dispositions of character required to make it through the journey. As with all rites of passage, there should always be a witness to your movement from one era of your life to another. My suggestion is that you invite everyone you possibly can. Naturally, your committee will be there already. On top of that, however, it may take some guts to invite others. You may already be nervous about presenting your findings, but I want to ask you to put on the goggles of one, five, or 10 years from now: Will the *you* five years from now wish that others had been present to witness this monumental "becoming" in your life? My suggestion is to get as many people into that room who love you and support you as humanly possible. Consider including the following individuals on your guest list:

1. Spouse and children;
2. Parents and extended family;
3. In-laws;
4. Cohort members and other fellow students;
5. Peers of the work, worship, and social natures;
6. Faculty members who have had a significant impact on you;
7. Local press (no, I'm not joking);
8. Entire online social sphere via Facebook® or YouTube® Live; and
9. Mentors.

Essentially, anyone who has supported you in your doctoral work and your ability to be there in that oral defense should be invited. You are crafting a ceremony. Still, if the norm of your university is to have only the committee present or to only have a virtual meeting for the purpose of the defense, defer to that. Regardless, ask your chair if you are welcome to invite others.

Become the host of your ceremony. While the chair's role is to moderate the discussion, maintain the agenda, and be the holder of the keys of the school's authority within the room, it's your role to prepare the physical environment in which the presentation will take place (whether it's a conference room at your university or a webinar "room"). After determining the date of your oral defense, reserve a location, order refreshments, and visit the site to see what the room will look like. Figure out how the furniture should be situated, how the equipment functions, if you need dongles or adapters for your laptop (I advise you to use your own computer), and what it feels like to project to an audience within the room. Contact your school's food vendor, cafeteria, or food services department and ask how much it would cost you to provide coffee service for the meeting along with pastry, snack, and finger food. Make reservations down the street at a local restaurant for the after-party for your guests. Ask a friend to video the meeting and discreetly take photos of you making your presentation. As you step into the final moments of your dissertation world, set the tone of the environment as one that exudes the gratitude and confidence within you. Make this a moment to remember for all concerned, and document yourself stepping across this final doctoral threshold.

52

SAY THANK YOU

In our book *Building the World's Greatest High School Student Leader,* Richard Parkhouse and I discuss the moments leading up to that final walk taken by students across the stage to get their diploma and to move on with the rest of their lives. We reflect on the power of anyone, even you as a soon-to-graduate doctoral student, stepping up onto that stage, looking back behind you at the whole of your life that has unfolded up until this point — especially the recent years leading to this grand moment — and being able to leave with no regrets.

Soon, oh so soon, the door of your life as a doctoral candidate will be shutting behind you, and you'll be crossing the threshold into a whole new era of *you.* What do you want to leave behind when you make that crossing? Is there something that you need to clean up before you move on? Is there something that needs to be said? To whom? These final moments are deeply precious, not just because you will look back at them with great warmth and appreciation but also because you'll be looking back to this moment as a point that marked a profound change in your life. You cannot traverse the land into which you are about to enter shackled to the regrets of the past — and not without giving deep, thoughtful, present thanks to your mentors, coaches, confidants, and friends for their help on this journey. The oral defense can be a ceremony of change — just like that "crossing" ritual that I described from my youth — where you not only take notice of your accomplishment and the impact that is about to have on your future but also acknowledge and thank those people who helped you along the journey. Don't leave that room until you have had the chance to say boldly, "Thank you!"

Consider your dissertation chair — the amount of time this person put forth in reviewing your drafts, speaking with you on the phone, listening to you as you vented about the difficulties that you were enduring, potentially duking it out with you when things were not going exactly smoothly, and helping you reorient yourself to the map of progress when all seemed lost. Chances are, your chair believed in you even when you did not. Your chair was sure about the potential and possibility of your finishing even when you were not entirely sure that you would ever finish. He or she probably refereed the committee, the administration, the IRB, and the quality review people on your behalf. Your chair spent time away from his or her family and spouse, for little pay or recognition, all to simply help you as a budding scholar to cross this threshold. What will you say to this person? What moments stick out to you in particular about the journey? What ritual object or talisman do you wish to leave with him or her upon your departure? Purchase something for your chair. You'll never regret it. Make it personal. It does not have to be fancy, but it has to be something symbolic of your time working with one another. Make it something worth keeping on a shelf and something that is accompanied by words of thanks — the type of thanks that has to be given with vulnerability.

Consider your spouse and your family. What sacrifices did they have to make so that you could be standing at your oral defense? What major moments in their life and yours were set aside so that you could conduct this research, write this paper, and finally finish? Think about the date nights missed, the intimate times sitting with one another placed on hold, and the evenings or mornings redirected to this undertaking. Think about those hundreds of hours. Think about the ways that they listened to you when you were having a hard time, when you were inspired about your obscure theoretical framework, and when you were learning about the statistical methods of *whatever*. What needs to be said to them in the room while everyone is listening to you and feeling the weight of this huge accomplishment? What gifts should be given? Should *time* be given back in spades? Should you have a vacation booked and ready to announce in your final presentation slide? Should you have the limo waiting outside? Should the plane tickets be bought? Should the BIG SURPRISE you've been fanaticizing about giving them finally come to fruition? You owe them a debt far greater than you know today — a debt you will come to know in the months and years to come when you have your feet finally back under you as a graduate. Remember: Heroes never return home the same as they left. Prepare your family to be with you on the next chapter of your journey.

Have words for your boss, your friends, your colleagues, and all the other people in your life who inspired you. Every person in that room should experience your eye contact, your voice saying his or her name, your direct, personal words of thanks about precise moments when he or she made an impact on you. Allow them to experience the weight of *their presence* within your life by recounting what their support has meant to you. Seriously, tell them specifics about what they did that was so impactful. Take photos with them. Assemble the whole group for a photo — everyone from your chair and your committee to your spouse, your friends, your boss, and your peers. Send out a copy of that photo to each and every single one of them with a thank-you card. Print the photo in large format, frame that thing, and put it in your workspace. You are about to close the door on an entire era of your life. The last page of the storybook always has an image of the final passage. What will your final page look like? Will you give yourself the gift of documenting these final moments, where you gave a symbolic bow to your allies and said, "From the bottom of my heart, thank you for you who are"?

53

DATE YOUR CHAIR

It's far easier to maintain a healthy relationship from the start than to revive a dying relationship after the damage has been done. Dysfunctional relationships between candidates and chairs are costly in terms of time and money and are entirely avoidable. Further, as I will later describe in this book, it's on you, the candidate, to create the ultimate conditions for a thriving relationship with your chair that will best foster your ability to finish. During this chapter, I will talk about the beginning stages of the chair-candidate relationship, before a formal deal to work together is struck, and the major working phases of your partnership. Later in this book, I'm going to talk about what to do when things go "bad."

I am one of the most fortunate men on the planet. I met a spouse who is one of the strongest women of this generation; she's a warrior. She has the heart of a lion. She's better with money than I am. She's far more patient than me. She's a great friend, spouse, partner, and mother of my kids. We are great together — and getting better every day. While I do often look into the cloudy sky here and thank God for His grace and providence of allowing me to have her in my life, I also attribute the health of Dr. Wife's and my relationship to the fact that we are very compatible: Our ways of being, seeing, and going with one another are *nearly entirely* complementary. If you are one of the fortunate candidates who's in a doctoral program that allows candidates to enter into an advising relationship with a faculty member of their choosing, you have a great deal of power in making a selection that will best help you finish. When you are in the early stages of your doctoral life, you can look for faculty members around you who share your interests, inspire you, have a way of mentoring that you admire, and have experience helping candidates through their dissertation. Prior to engaging potential chairs in any discussion, before you corner them on a break and talk at them for 15 minutes about your dissertation while they go glassy-eyed, before you send them a 30-page draft, have your eyes open to the kind of chair they could be. Download dissertations they chaired. Track down fellow candidates, if possible, who currently work with the chairs and ask about their experience. If applicable, read the feedback that these faculty members provide you in some of your courses. Assess the busyness of the individuals. Ask yourself, (1) Do they already interact with me in a way that I admire? (2) Do they provide feedback to me already that is helpful? (3) Do they seem like they will have the time necessary to guide me through this process of finishing my dissertation? After you have adequately considered a few possible chairs and have written a great introductory chapter or concept paper (seriously, don't skip that part), and once your program allows you to reach out formally to potential chairs, you're ready to take the formal step of interviewing potential chairs. Before you do that, though, always come to a conclusion: "Why is this the faculty member who can best help me when things get *really* tough?"

Lucky candidates will attend programs that have "meet the chairs," "chair speed-dating," or "advancement interview" events where they are placed in an environment specifically designed for the purpose of finding a dissertation chair. Less fortunate candidates will have to make time outside formal course time to interact with potential chairs. This could require travel, carefully written emails, and sober phone calls. Regardless, this is where your formal "dating" relationship begins, where you need to ask all the questions required to make an informed decision about which of the many possible faculty members who could chair your committee is mutually a best fit: a fit for the position of chair and compatible with you, the student. Your chair will want you to finish! Also, you want to finish! Here are some questions you'll want to ask:

1. What is your process when working with candidates?

2. Are you "hands on," "hands off," or something in between?

3. What do you expect of your candidates?

4. How do you deliver feedback?

5. How quickly do you respond to emails?

6. How long is the typical wait to receive feedback on a draft?

7. What type of doctoral student is your ideal candidate?

8. Can you help me figure out how long it might take me to finish my dissertation? (See Chapter 44)

9. Would you be willing to take a look at my introductory chapter and tell me what you see?

The answers to these questions can offer you the chance to understand what a potential chair wants and if that is compatible with your desires.

Once a formal relationship is struck, you and your chair should have a firm agreement on when and how your interactions will occur. When is your next iteration of your dissertation due to your chair? How long will it take him or her to return feedback once that draft is received? When is it appropriate or required to initiate face-to-face or voice-to-voice interaction? Precisely, what is your next step with one another? Protect the health of your relationship with your chair like you would a relationship with a loved spouse. Read your emails out loud and hear yourself: Do you sound like the kind of person with whom you would want to work? Keep your relationship thriving.

———————————————

54

GIVE ALL REQUIRED FOR AN EASY YES

Sitting on this side of the dissertation, I know that I could go back and complete a dissertation quite quickly. It's akin to the feeling you have when you speak to someone much younger who has just had the first major heartbreak of his or her life: You've been there, you know what this person is going through, feel for him or her, and know everything is going to be okay. You know this person's potential missteps. You saw the warning signs. It's with hindsight that you have the brand of wisdom that comes with experience. On this side of the dissertation, I know that your university probably has *already* made available everything that you need to succeed in this process. In your situation, it very much may not feel like that. You are seeing the barriers in front of you. It's possible you and your chair have a dysfunctional relationship. You are feeling the challenges of meeting the reading and writing timeframes that have been put in front of you — and those that are lurking in your brain when you attempt to sit and simply enjoy a cup of tea or glass of wine at the end of the night. You're afraid that if you don't get moving on this thing in a serious way, you'll never finish. All these feelings are normal, and sometimes they can shield you from seeing that you already have at your fingertips all that you need to undertake and finish this journey. As you begin to pivot through the major benchmarks of your dissertation writing, including the (1) initial concept paper, (2) proposal draft and defense, (3) IRB application, (4) final chapter writing and oral defense, and (5) final clean-up edits, please remember that the human beings involved in these processes need specific items from you. My recommendation is to not only provide them with what they need, but, to the best of your ability, always overdeliver on what's expected. Make all yeses as painless as possible.

Remember, revisions will nearly always be requested, but I would prefer you have minor revisions rather than major ones. I'd much rather you avoid rewriting your entire literature review chapter. I want you to avoid having the organization supporting your data collection suddenly decide you're "too risky" to work with. I want your character and the quality of your work to show the hard work you have endured to create a product ready to be showcased. So, as you approach each of these major stages in your dissertation writing, consider three ways in which you can ensure that everything is present that is required for an easy "yes" — because "YES" is what I want you to hear!

First, regularly download the latest dissertation guide from your program. Most programs have such guides, templates, checklists, etc. that are to be used by candidates to form the basic framework of their writing. These are regularly updated. You're typically responsible for all revisions mandated by such guides while you are in the dissertation writing phase. Some universities even have complicated (and sometimes quite large) rubrics that are to be used by the dissertation chairs for their work with candidates. If you have a developed (or perhaps overdeveloped) quality review apparatus at your university, these guides will be particularly important, as it's often the quality reviewers, paid methodologists, and head research faculty who write these in the first place. Truly, I'm seeing quality reviewers often operating as the "final authority" of these dissertation committees because they have the power to exert tremendous authority. Supplicate to the gods of quality review: Give them what they want from the start. As best you can from the start, write your dissertation drafts within the established format mandated by your university. When you are ready to submit, double-check again and again that you have met those requirements. In my experience, one of the worst situations is losing months of writing time (especially) based on technicalities.

Second, consult the IRB (ethics) application for your university/program early on in your dissertation writing and continue to consult it throughout your drafting process. You'll notice that this application asks exceedingly specific questions about your data collection and analysis procedures, how you will be approaching potential participants (if any), and how you plan on ensuring informed consent and confidentiality. Early on, this application is very useful in that it walks you through all the questions you should be asking yourself about your study. You'll have the chance to answer the questions that are asked within your actual dissertation draft and in the attached appendices. Later on, it will be expected that your dissertation's contents are in concert with the IRB application. If and when the IRB has additional questions for you regarding your procedures, this can be *very* costly in terms of time. Some IRBs only meet monthly. Sometimes, during summer months in particular, IRBs may only meet every six to 12 weeks. If you're a lucky doctoral student, your IRB operates on a rolling basis year-long.

Finally, your assisting faculty (including your committee members) *will* provide feedback for your drafts. It's possible that you will feel like the feedback is not robust enough! This is when you need to get on the phone (yes, that thing that involves the use of your voice) and talk with them about their requests and concerns. It's up to you to do this! They will rarely initiate this step for you! Voice is where clarifications can be much more comprehensive and deep than via written format. Additionally, when working with quality review, you may discover that the reviewers are not directly available to speak, as many universities utilize blind reviewers and methodologists who cannot directly interact with candidates (which I personally think is a bit silly). You'll have to rely heavily on your chair during these moments to understand the feedback provided. Respond to every feedback request without fail, knowing fully what the reviewers want of you.

55

IT'S NOT THEIR FAULT

Every candidate has experienced frustration of some kind with his or her chair. However, there is a level of frustration that goes so deep and expands to such a level that a doctoral candidate may stop working altogether. When I meet with candidates who have been ABD for more than three years and the focus of our conversation revolves around their chair's work, I'm greatly saddened for such dissertation writers because the focus of their anger is usually entirely misplaced. You can't blame your gym for your failure to get fit. You can't blame your stove for your body fat percentage. You can't blame your radio for making you feel bad. You can't entirely blame your boss for your performance. You can't blame your dissertation chair for your inability to make progress. Unless something illegal or unethical is happening in your relationship with that chair, at the risk of being very controversial, I assure you, your chair has little to do with your failure to complete a writing and research project — even one as monumental as this dissertation. If negative energy toward your chair is the focus of your dissertation-related energies, you're entirely on the wrong path, and if nothing changes, you'll never finish.

In the ultimate fashion, your chair can be a mentor of writing, spirit, body, and mind — one who is shaping you into the scholar practitioner that you undoubtedly *could* be. Your chair can be the type of leader who cares about you in the ways that you need most, even if that means having to piss you off from time to time to get you moving. Your chair can be the type of role model you hope to emulate. Your chair may represent ideals to you as a human being — ideals that not only help you through this difficult season of finishing but that also truly define you as a mother, sister, student, worker, and whole person. Your chair might be quite charismatic in his or her way of interacting with the world. This individual could be a deal-maker on your behalf or a negotiator with you to bargain your way toward meeting the goals you mutually set forth. Your chair might be deeply collaborative, conservative, and caring. Like having the ideal coach on your side to help foster some major life transformation — almost like choosing a mentor to help you become a body-builder, martial artist, or musician — you could have the kind of chair who wants to deeply partner with you. You'll be greatly blessed by such a chair. You'll never forget him or her. You'll consider naming your child or family pet after your chair. At the very least, you'll thank this individual in the acknowledgement section of your dissertation. You might have this type of chair.

On the other hand, you might have the type of chair whom you've never met in person. You might have a chair who does not answer emails. Your chair may only provide cursory feedback like, "Good job; keep going," and then call you on lots of mistakes when you submit a draft later on. Your chair may take eight or more weeks to send you any feedback at all. He or she may take unannounced vacations. He or she may have said flat out to your face, "I don't think you're ever going to finish." Your chair may ask you to change your methodology, change your purpose statement, or change your topic (again), and may completely contradict something that he or she said in a previous conversation. Unless your chair is doing something that could get him or her fired or arrested, none of this person's actions have an impact on your ability to, in the end, finish your dissertation. The lack of support may cost you time, energy, funds, and lots of tears, but you are not "trapped" by your chair's actions. It's not your chair's fault. You can't blame him or her. You not only can't do that, but you shouldn't blame your chair even if you could. Don't give in to the powers of darkness that want you to feel like there is no way out. Everything — *everything* — is workable.

Think about some of the most difficult moments you have endured as a human being. Could you have endured these things alone? One thing that many candidates don't realize is that they are *not* alone, even when it truly feels like they are.

It's true that if your chair is the only dissertation-related person in your life, you could be alone! But it does not have to be that way. My community of doctoral learners in The Dissertation Mentor® Accelerator Program are experiencing many of the challenges that you experience each day. There are dozens of other faculty members at your university and abroad who willingly will engage with you in your writing and research, because that's what great scholars do: They help one another. There are dozens of books and texts about writing, methodology, research, and self-help. There are editors, experts, and entrepreneur-scholars (like me) who are willing to help. You don't have to be alone in your frustration and let your progress stop there *forever*.

When your negative attention turns to your chair, feeling like it's his or her fault that you are not making progress, remember that unless something illegal or unethical is happening, this energy is a complete waste of your time. You're getting angry at your cigarette for causing cancer. Put down that emotion, look at it on the table in front of you, and say, "Okay, anger, negativity, trappedness, frustration, etc., I see you! What are you trying to tell me? What can I do to take the necessary personal and academic steps forward?" In my experience, the answers to these questions often circulate into considering what YOU can do *today*, right now, to make some progress. The answers include (1) downloading and printing one study, (2) reading one study, (3) making some highlights on one study, (4) writing down five useful quotes from a source, or (5) finding one friend, peer, or mentor and talking about your study (without griping) for five minutes. Turn frustration into movement. Frustration will try to hold you in place when you need to move.

56

IT'S NOT A DEGREE – IT'S A TRANSFORMATION

The journey is the goal; your dissertation is the path. Beyond that final oral defense, degree posting, and graduation is something (or someone) that is calling for you. The point of this process is not just to write a paper. You did not wake up one morning six years ago and say, "Gee, I *really* want to write a dissertation." You sensed a calling of some kind. Many of you reading this already have a profound sense of what that calling is; you know where you are headed and what might be possible for you. Some of you have no idea what's ahead. This project may be clouding your vision to such a degree that you can only see the laptop screen in front of your face. You are being prepared for something that lies beyond the threshold of *finishing*. You are not simply preparing a dissertation; you are preparing for that reality that lies beyond. Big stuff is coming. Truly, you have no idea how grand it will be. You have no idea the opportunities that will open for you and the opportunities that will be coming to find you! All of this hard work is a preparation. You are undergoing a transformation into the person you will need to be to face the next challenges that wait beyond that final threshold. Remembering the relationship between this writing project and what's coming will infuse you with energy. You are not making something; you are becoming something.

You are transforming into one who writes as a scholar. Your writing professors probably said to you at one point, "Where is the citation for this sentence?" You learned early on in your writing process that you were not allowed to speak from your own experience and your own intuition in your writing of the dissertation.

257

This probably came as a huge shock; after all, we all work in environments that are permeated by anecdote, personal reflection, and stories of "a time when" *whatever*. Some of us even work and operate in places where "The research says" is thrown around like some sort of tennis ball — no sources named, no studies mentioned, but "the research says" *something*. You are learning that to get your ideas onto paper in a way that is acceptable in scholarly circles, you have to be prepared for the rigor of peer review and the challenges that will come from that. You need to mention your sources. You can't simply get a pass because you sound smart. You have to cite others who have done the hard work of research or grand practice before you. You are going to be the type of person whose words are backed up by the weight of tested evidence, not simply the gripes of one who's "been there, done that" through the tests of experience.

You are also transforming into a scholarly practitioner. Through the powers of research and action that you are gaining, you are becoming a person of practice who applies the findings and methods of research into your daily work. You are becoming the type of leader in your field who is willing to test, develop, and implement solutions that are going to be of some major benefit to humanity. To do this, you are learning how how others are conducting research and how to go about doing that in your own line of practice. In writing this book, for example, I surveyed thousands of people to discover what major challenges they were facing in their dissertation work. I did not invent this out of the clouds between my ears; I utilized the same skills that I developed in my research to apply to my own life. Further, as one who is reading scholarship and engaging with other scholars, you are learning much that can be applied to your daily work and those you serve. You are becoming a master in a way because the masters are always learning, always advancing, always deepening as practitioners themselves. The fruit of your practice can become more clear as your practice becomes more precise.

Most important to me, personally, is that you are becoming an authentic "doer." You are becoming a practitioner in this thing called "your life." You have decided that you are not going to sit on your couch with a bag of potato chips and simply slog on at your place of employment until your bosses get tired of you or allow you to retire. You are not waiting for that government subsidy check to arrive when it's time to stop leaving the house every day to earn a living. You are the type of human being who has set your mind to do something, and by the grace of God, you're going to do it, *darn it!* You are becoming the type of person who is willing to set your alarm clock earlier, go to bed sooner, eat more healthfully, and drink a fair amount of water to keep your mind clear. You are becoming the type of person who is learning that certain types of entertainment are distracting you from the good work that you could be doing and even, days or hours after the fact, can have a detrimental impact on your emotions. You are transforming into the brand of human being who can draw on your various capacities and resources to get something *huge* done — and undertake a monumental life transformation along the way. You are becoming like those wise guys and gals of old — the people who have made a major splash in this world because they dared to undertake a personal change drastically out of sync with the rest of society. You are becoming the type of person who is willing to not take the easy path; you've chosen one of the most challenging paths that you possibly could because you know that this is the one that holds the promise of the transformation you seek. When things get hard, when things fall apart, always return to this sense of *becoming*. You are becoming someone. You are transforming into someone. As Tennyson wrote, speaking for Ulysses, you are "[becoming] a name!" Know that everything you are going through today is in service of this transformation.

WHEN THINGS FALL APART

In this section, I'll give you some strategies to employ during the hard times and some ways to appreciate the good ones.

57

LOST IN MY LITERATURE REVIEW

There are times within your dissertation process when you feel like you are under a pile of bricks — or books. It's as if you are drowning. You can't see how far you have come, or worse yet, you feel like you have gone nowhere at all. One of the most challenging times that I see candidates experiencing these emotions is when they are climbing the mountain of the literature review. After all, it's one of the largest chapters, requiring the greatest amount of time and personal investment, and when your chair asks for a major revision, this can be a major trauma. It's often at this stage that candidates freeze. When students live in a state of perpetual ABD, it's often in the literature review work. I can *nearly* guarantee that if you are able to conquer the literature review to such a degree that your chair (and your quality review team) agrees that you are done, you have completed about 60% or more of your dissertation work already. After all, what's after? A straightforward methodology chapter, some arduous data collection, and the grand finale of discussing your findings. I'm so radically passionate about this topic that I dedicated nearly a third of this book to it, and a great deal of my online courses relate to this topic. So, if you are feeling lost here, know three things:

First, know that you are not alone. It always strikes me how many candidates wallow in the emotional state of "There must be something wrong with me" if they find themselves caught up in the ardors of the literature review. Just like your introductory sessions (or months) in a rigorous exercise program, the literature review will continue to wind you until you win it. It's going to take lots of daily practice to be able to meet this challenge. Frankly, everyone who is reading this chapter — *EVERYONE* — has faced significant challenges in writing the literature review of his or her dissertation. You have to remember that the amount of work required to access hundreds of sources, read and annotate them all, and pull from them hundreds more pertinent quotes and tidbits of information is not easy for anybody. No one gets an easy pass in this part of the work. Everyone has to pay dues, and that is what you are doing if you feel yourself caught up in this part of the process. So, your only job is to pay your dues. Do that and you'll finish.

Second, know that the dues that you have to pay to finish this literature review are *very* straightforward. As I outlined in some of the earlier chapters of this text, there are a number of steps of practice that you need to take regularly, without fail, to conduct your literature review. You need to take at least five minutes today and download or reserve five texts of some kind related to the topics of your study. If you don't know where to start, look at your purpose statement and underline the nouns that you see. Search for those inside your favorite database. You need to get those resources into your hands. At another sitting, SKIM one of those sources. Highlight or flag sections that you think would be useful to read more fully. Go onto another source and another and another until you feel done for the day. At yet another sitting, go back to those flagged texts and read them in depth; highlight those quotes that you think may be useful in your work. Again, at yet another sitting, spend as much time as you can transferring all the highlights into a matrix like the one I described earlier in this book. Always strive to find at least five useful quotes in each text that is pertinent to your work. Keep doing this until you have 400-500 quotes spread between all your various theory areas named in your purpose statement. This is no small task, but it is not a complicated task. Notice that *nothing* about paying these dues mentioned in this paragraph is about writing; it's about spending the time required to do all the reading and pre-work in preparation for the writing. If you're not willing to do the prewriting steps, think about that for a couple months and then consider quitting school; save yourself the money. The reading and prewriting can't be skipped. Pay your dues.

Finally, know that the greatest trap that you will face is your own psyche's desire to hold onto the gains it has already made. This is where the pervasive disease of "I've already written this part" holds candidates back from going and doing the prewriting steps required. They feel like they have already written 30 pages and should not have to go back to the prewriting steps. They say things in their heads like, "If I can only make my chair happy and make these major edits inside what I've already done, I won't have to do a full rewrite." Often, they fail to see that the whole reason that their chair is asking them for these edits is because they failed to do the prewriting steps — all that reading, annotating, gathering, and synthesizing — in the first place. These candidates sat with a Microsoft® Word window open alongside a browser window, transferring information from one online source into their dissertation directly. They tried to skip the prewriting steps. Know that it would be far easier to go back and do all the prewriting steps fresh than to try to edit a bad literature review into health. Remember, you are not writing a literature review; you are conducting one. If you are deeply lost at the literature review step and "have already written one," I recommend going back to the start and beginning fresh. You probably already have piles of articles ready for this step. All you have to do is read them, annotate them, pop them into your matrix, and prepare for the steps of using those lines of text to create the awesome outline of your best final product possible. Know that feeling lost in your literature review is usually a call to go back to basics: read, annotate, collect, synthesize, outline, write, rewrite.

58

THE SUN IS NOT BROKEN

This year, my family moved to Portland, Oregon, the fulfillment of a lifelong dream for me and my family. When I was about 10 years old, my dad lost his job. It was a major turning point for him at 50 years old and caused a great deal of emotional and spiritual shifts within my family. Imagine working your whole life toward being something, but then something happens that makes you wonder, "Is this really the thing that I am supposed to be doing?" Imagine going through that at 50 with a 10-year-old and an eight-year-old and a wife and a mortgage. One summer, we all got into the truck with a fifth-wheel trailer attached and just started driving. We ended up all kinds of places. We saw the Grand Canyon. We saw the Petrified Forest. We saw the forests of the Pacific Northwest. One day, we ended up in Oregon, perhaps one of the greenest, wettest places in the United States. I remember the exhalation of the wind through the trees when we arrived one night in the cold by the lake at Stewart State Park. Most summers after that until I was near finishing high school, we ended up driving north from California to Oregon and spending much of our time relaxing among the trees while my dad looked for work. In the months in between summers when we would be at home in California, my dad took odd jobs swinging a hammer. In the eight years until I turned 18 and moved out of my parents' house, we could never figure out how to get out. Oregon became a bit of the Promised Land for me. It was the place that my family could never reach and the one that I hoped I could get to one day after I paid off my student loans and did enough work for "the man." Just a handful of months ago, we finally did it. Most days, I get to do my writing looking out at a grove of trees next to a field of deep green grass, the white and dark grey billowing clouds rolling above often giving way to rain. It's a place of movement; nature is reminding me with her dance the way of things: always changing, dynamic, working.

Dissertation writers can often feel terribly trapped, stuck in a place where nothing seems workable. Depression and anxiety can hold you captive in two very different prisons. Depression is a slow, wallowing, sticky, low-energy, cold partner that wants you to sit and do nothing. He says to you with complete loss, "What is the point anyway?" If he has his way with you, you'll keep paying those continuation units to your university forever. You'll never finish. You'll never get the satisfaction of finishing — or the sense of closure if you decided to walk away. Often, this form of depression holds dissertation writers captive for years. In the lightest form, it could be a bit of procrastination. In the worst, one can experience clinical depression that requires an intervention by a professional. On the other hand, anxiety is a fast-working, high-energy, risk management attorney that wants to keep you safe and free from liabilities but does so by giving you so much to think about — or, at least, so much to worry about — that you don't complete those dissertation-related items. This guy wants you to focus your energy on all the metaphorical fires in your life. He speaks in the language of "what if." He will cloud your mind and agenda with other things besides dissertation writing; he may try to get you to take unethical shortcuts that could get you expelled, or he will raise your blood pressure, bring on panic attacks, or worse and cause you to need to seek out expert help. While I can't speak to the professional side of things (because I'm not a licensed physician or therapist), I can speak to you from my own experience: Much of what your brain is saying to you that is keeping you from your dissertation work is a lie, fake news, not worth your time. The biggest lie of them all is that nothing can change. If you hear that, you know that your brain is feeding you crap.

Everything is workable. Having ample opportunity in my new state of residence, I look up to the sky often and watch those clouds roll by. It can be quite dark, and some say it can be quite depressing, but the sun is still up there, beautiful people. It's just behind some atmospheric phenomena. Likewise, your dissertation writing can feel quite hopeless. It's possible that you have circumstances in your life that feel entirely unworkable, unchangeable, unmanageable. However, you are still here reading this page. You are still a breathing human being. Take a breath; if you can do that, there is still hope. Life is still moving, and if you keep rolling with the life-related phenomena buzzing around you, change is inevitable. For it to be the type of change that you want, however, you may need to take some radical actions. Some people in my life have often said, "Start small and make small changes." I often think that the best antidote to a feeling of being "stuck" is to GO BIG and do something crazy productive to get unstuck. If you find yourself in one of these dark places where you don't feel like anything could change, I want you to do something big to show yourself that change is possible. If you believe you are clinically depressed or anxious, seek the help of a medical or psychological professional — but in absence of that, I have a few ideas to help show you that you can change things and get some dissertation stuff done. These include downloading one article and hitting print; skimming one article for five minutes and making highlights; printing your one-sentence purpose statement on a piece of paper and hanging it on your bathroom mirror; typing one sentence you think is worthwhile from an article into a Microsoft® Excel spreadsheet; cleaning one table or desk that needs it; taking 60 minutes by yourself to eat a good meal at a local restaurant, tasting each bite of your food; and telling one person in your life what you are going through right now and asking that person if he or she would be willing to listen to you talk about it from time to time. The sun is not broken; there are simply some clouds rolling through.

59

CHAIR-SPLOSION

As a university-employed dissertation committee chair, there were times that I failed my candidates: Sometimes I did not answer emails in a timely fashion, sometimes I did not provide the comprehensive feedback needed for my candidates to succeed, and sometimes I was not clear in what I was communicating. However, in my own defense, these were minor and rare moments within my overall work with my candidates, mostly when my wife and I were bringing new babies into the world every 18-24 months for a few years. Largely, my work is characterized by clarity, a great deal of support, and a high level of investment in guiding my candidates across the finish line. The VAST MAJORITY of chairs fall into this category of professionals of which I am part; you'd want to work with us! Still there is a very, *very* small minority of chairs out there about whom there may be deep professional, ethical, and legal concerns. You may be working with such a chair. Here are some of the warning signs:

1. Habitual absence via email, via phone, or in person;

2. Habitual nonexistent, inaccurate, or inappropriate feedback;

3. Habitual inappropriate or unprofessional communication; or

4. Any other habitual, pervasive pattern of unprofessional behavior as a chair.

Sometimes, but even more rarely, some chairs engage in unethical practices such as requiring candidates to purchase their books or pay them for editorial services or consulting services outside of the university. Lastly, in the rarest of cases (none of which I have personally ever encountered), some chairs may engage in illegal behavior. When problems arise with your chair (keeping in mind what I said back in Chapter 55), ask yourself, "Is this something that could be considered (1) unprofessional, (2) unethical, or (3) illegal?" If you believe that your chair's behavior falls into one of the last two categories, stop reading this book and seek the help of your university's administration. In the case where you see your chair as operating unprofessionally, there are a few questions to consider.

First, if your chair is acting unprofessionally, ask yourself, "To what degree is this my fault?" While you may laugh or scowl at the page as I write this, it's worth saying that nearly all candidates will find themselves angry with their chair at some point. To what degree are you contributing to the situation at hand? If your chair is consistently having difficulty communicating with you, you might play some part in that; you might not. However, depending on where this journey toward rectifying this situation with your chair might go, it's best to spend a short amount of time reflecting on your part in the communication challenges that have arisen between you and your chair.

Second, ask yourself if you are willing (if it is possible) to fix this situation with your chair. If the experience has gone so sour that you cannot stand working with this person another day, you know that you will need to go through formal channels to make a change of chairs. At some universities, you'll have to say why the change is being made, and you'll need to decide the degree to which you're willing to mention the dynamics with your chair that are leading you to this decision. These conversations around switching chairs can have an impact on your program administration's view of both you and your chair. Walk with caution when things like this have gone bad and you want to make a change. If you are willing to continue to work with your chair, provided that the situation improves, then proceed by asking the following question.

Next, to what degree can you name the specific ways of working together that need to be changed? Can you create a list of the specific ways of interacting between you two that need to change? What specifically do you need from this chair? Within how many days do you need your chair to reply to your emails? Within how many days do you need your chair to return comprehensive feedback for a draft submission? How many times can you expect your chair to provide such feedback for a specific area, section, or chapter of your draft? After how many tries do you, personally, feel responsible for getting it right? What are the preferred ways of communicating with your chair? Email? Phone? In person? When will you need to have interactions with your chair for the foreseeable season to come? Can you make a list of these requests, demands, or hopes so that you can communicate them with your chair when the time comes?

Finally, consider seriously googling "nonviolent communication" and "crucial conversations"; read up on how to navigate situations such as these when conflict arises between two human beings, and be a model candidate in your cordial, professional email, asking if your chair could meet with you via phone or in person to discuss your future work with one another. If your chair doesn't answer after a week, send him or her another cordial email asking, "Did you get my previous email?" If your chair still doesn't answer after another week, start calling him or her on the phone. If he or she doesn't return your call after another week, it may be time to reach out with a concerned tone to your administration, asking, "Is Dr. So-and-so okay? I emailed her a few times and even called a couple times in the past month and am hearing nothing back." Remember, even if your chair is being unprofessional, that does not give you license to be anything less than the ultimate doctoral candidate. In the end, you may need to change chairs, but try to keep that as a last resort.

60

THE PHD AUDACITY

When I was about nine years old, I sat weekly in Sunday School hearing about those storied "heroes of the Bible" whom nearly any of us today, regardless of our creed or culture, could name. One day, probably when hearing about Moses, Joseph, Noah, or one of the Old-Testament prophets, a question came to my mind: "I wonder what all the other people in the world were doing at this time?" When hearing the story of the crucifixion of Jesus, I often wondered about the poor office worker down the road from Golgotha in Hellenistic Judah who simply got up in the morning and decided to get cracking on his work, ignoring the mob following a cross-carrying Christ. He probably looked at the work piling up in his inbox and said, "Wow, I really would love to go out there to see what all this commotion is about, but man, my boss is going to kill me if I don't get this done." This gave me some serious perspective on the growing amount of homework that I was forced to endure during my elementary school years. Early on, I became very interested in the idea that there were certain people who were mentioned in ancient texts and millions (and billions) of others who were not. Over time, I've come to find that everyone — *everyone* — undertakes a heroic journey in life of some kind. Everyone, for a time, leaves the metaphorical village, learns something new, faces dragons, and then returns home with new skills and a calling to live a new way. Still, there are people who do something truly rare, something worthy of notice. You are doing that type of work if you have the audacity to pursue a Ph.D., Ed.D., LMNOP, or doctor of *whatever*. You are doing something that is unlike 99% of what the population is doing. Acknowledging that you are doing something monumentally rare can be a great help when difficulties arise. There are some people who will stay home today and not do the work they feel the calling to complete. You've already answered the call!

When things fall apart, remember that you are already on a path that few walk and that you probably cannot hold yourself to the same measures to which you have always held yourself. When you are up at 5:00 a.m. trying to squeeze in some exercise or some literature review reading, annotating, or organizing, think about what 90% or more of the population is doing at this very minute in your area: They are dead asleep. When you are spending those lunch breaks searching ProQuest® Database for some new, tasty articles, remember that the average person is browsing the web, talking with a dear friend, or spending time enjoying the outdoors. When you spend time away from family, time that you truly miss, and feel that you may regret it one day, remember that you are doing something that few do. The old measures of getting a good night's sleep for eight or more hours (if that ever happened for you), spending a certain number of hours with your family, or dedicating yourself, as you always have, to your job may not be attainable for a season. Your measures of what is acceptable, worthwhile, and healthy need to be adjusted for a season. Like a prizefighter who radically adjusts his or her eating habits for a desired goal near the time of a match, you too are taking up a season of work that is radical and rare. New measures are needed. First, think about the task in front of you: How many sources will you find each day? How many sources will you read each day? How many will you annotate? How many quotes will you always endeavor to pull from each source? Second, think about all the people you love in your life: Who makes the list? How much time can you dedicate to each person on this list each week? Finally, think of all your other commitments; list them on a piece of paper. Take your commitments in writing your dissertation, your goals there, your list of loved ones, and calendar out the typical weekday. What do you need to do each day? Create measures that can give you an easy "yes" or "no" about whether you're on track. If you can say, "Yes, I hit all my checkboxes for the day in terms of reading one source, annotating one source, pulling five quotes from that reading, getting X done at work, and spending Y minutes speaking with those I love today," you'll feel better about the insane rarity of your situation.

Humility, authentically seeing and acknowledging how charmed your life is, will help you far more than any other tip I've given you in this book. The fact that you have the pleasure of waking up with electricity, running water, a toilet, access to food and clean water, internet access, and a semi-functioning government, with the health, wealth, and chance to attend a university and gain the highest level of education it offers, makes you one of the luckiest people on the planet. If, on top of that, you have a healthy and loving family surrounding you, a boss who supports you, and a stable (or even thriving) mode of employment, you are among the rarest of the rare. You could have been born before the advent of modern dentistry. You could have been born a caveman in sub-Saharan Africa before recorded history. You've already won the lottery of life. All you have to do is the hard work to cash in on your winnings. Frankly, I get scared for my kids: Will they have the opportunities that I have had during my lifetime? Do you ever have the same concerns? Likewise, when I look at the world around me and all that I want to get done in my life, when I look at my aging face in the mirror and think about all those colleagues of mine who died before their time, and when I look at my kids — holy God, when I look at my kids — I wonder, will the opportunities that I have in my hands today always be present? It's up to you and me to have the fortitude to run headlong into the storm of life and become what we are being called to be while we can.

61

IS IT WORTH IT?

Pursuing this thing is audacious enough, and then you begin to look at your family, your coworkers, and the whole of what you could be doing in the world, asking, "Is writing this thing worth it?" There is no dissertation writer who has not had this question cross his or her mind at some time in the long climb from topic to literature review, to full-on study, to data collection, through data analysis, and finally to presentation and defense. In this chapter, I want to spend a moment saying to you that *it is worth it*. As I just said in the previous chapter, you've won the lottery of life if you are able to spend any moment of your thoughts meditating on the possibilities of undertaking the highest academic pursuit available on the planet. When things get really hard, *really challenging*, I want you to think about some of the ways that this doctoral degree is going to place a massive mark in the history of your life and the lives of so many others. You are not just doing this thing for you; you're doing it for lots of other people too. Let's chat about you first and then let's talk about them.

In a short number of months or years, with a great deal of hard work and discipline, you are going to be done with your doctoral degree. Doors will open to you that you do not yet even know exist. You are going to get emails from people you've never met asking for your assistance in their research, in their writing projects, with their business, or even offering you a job. You are going to be seen entirely differently by many of your peers at work, in your family, and at your place of worship. You are going to be seen as a huge resource to many and a threat to some.

Lots of people are going to look at you with admiration while others are going to look at you with contempt, neither group fully understanding what it is that you did to get those letters behind your name. If you are an educator like me working with high school-age or younger students, you'll garner a deep respect from many of their parents — and, like I experienced, you may have a parent ask you about a growth on her neck before you have the chance to explain you are not that type of doctor. You are going to get access to positions and opportunities in leadership, teaching, entrepreneurship, interpreneurship, and innovation that only could be accessed by the doctoral version of you. All that is about to happen. All you have to do is finish. The best, however, comes from those whom you get to serve through your accomplishment and engagement as a scholarly practitioner after graduation.

The children in your family, if there are any, from your kids to those of your siblings and beyond, will have a redefined sense of what is possible for them. I know that my children will live a very different life because their mother and I both finished the doctoral journey. A high standard is set, and they can see how we came so far to make that a reality for our lives. It's possible that you've lived a far less charmed life than I have and have already endured far more than I ever had to. Will your family not be even more empowered by the length and depth of your crazy journey toward finishing your doctoral degree? Think about the children of these children and beyond. You are causing a shockwave of educational possibility through their lives. Further, as one who has undergone the mental (and even spiritual) transformation that scholarship provides, you will have new ways of engaging with your family, helping them to discover a new way of exploring questions, new ideas, and new ways of interacting with the world. As a friend of my family's once expressed to us as children, "When there is a fire in the forest, more than one tree burns." Yes, you are getting a doctoral degree, but your family will undergo that transformation with you. They are in it with you.

Lastly, consider those you will serve through the newfound opportunities that will further reveal themselves in the years to come. As someone who is completing a dissertation, it's possible that you are already giving a voice to those who have not yet had a voice in the matters you are exploring. It's possible that you are serving as the mouthpiece of the oppressed, the stressed, and the overworked, among many others who could finally have a published voice through your written words. As someone who is completing a dissertation, you are forwarding the work of other researchers who have come before you. You are advancing the cause of your topic in your field. You are sharpening practice and helping others be far more impactful in the work they do each day. Accordingly, by extension, you are helping all the people who will be served by your research directly and indirectly. The nurses, for example, who may read your study and learn to work more empathetically with their patients are not the only ones to benefit; the patients, their families, and those who will come after them will also greatly benefit. Further, as you graduate, take on new positions, do some creative or innovative activity inside or outside your place of employment, and potentially continue your scholarship, you will help more and more of those whom you serve in ways that you never could have before you completed this doctoral transformation. A brand of warriorship that has interested me greatly these past eight years has been that of waking up to the maximum extent so that I can help others wake up. May you do just that with those you serve; may the fruition of your efforts as a doctoral dissertation writer edge you further and further toward being the ultimate servant so that all of those served can become the ultimate servants for others in their lives. When things get hard, remember that you are not just doing this for you. The whole world may be counting on you to become the person you are meant to be.

62

LEAVING YOUR CHILD IN THE WILDERNESS

There may come a time when you need to walk away, a time when you decide that this doctoral path is not for you. There may come a set of circumstances of life that will not allow you to finish. It's possible that you might change your mind about completing the doctoral degree altogether. Emotionally, when I think about walking away from a prized creative project, one in which I have invested years of time, brainpower, stress, and finances, it can feel for me like something as terrible as leaving my child in the wilderness. When you are up to your ears in difficulty or so much hardship has arisen in your life that you have ignored the dissertation altogether for an extended period of time, if you are thinking about not finishing, you have to ask yourself one question: "Will I feel regret about giving up on my dissertation and on my doctoral journey?" Think about the short-term, the coming weeks and months: How will you feel about this decision then? What about in five or 10 years? To what degree might you regret the decision to stay or the decision to walk away later in life? If you feel a great sense of potential for regret, as if you had abandoned your own kid in the forest, then you are probably not yet ready to give up. You never want to leave with regret, like having a bad ending to a relationship. If you are going to leave, you need to leave as if you had your blessing to do so — as much as possible, the guilt-free license to go on living your life doing something else. It's best to walk away based on a decision, not with a sense of absolute defeat. Still, as I write this, I know what you are feeling; I too am feeling the sense of taboo, remorse, regret, and failure that swirls around this topic.

The vast majority of doctoral programs and their faculty will counsel you about how to "keep going," and here I am talking about when you might want to give up. There are times in life, however, that warrant walking away from your dissertation. Just like the culture in the United States has largely accepted that there are some circumstances in which it's completely okay to leave a bad marriage (while for hundreds of years divorce was such a taboo), I want to be a voice of sanity here that tells you there are times when it's okay to walk away from your dissertation. The caveat to all this is that I want you to not rely solely on my words as backup for your decision; if you decide to leave your doctoral studies, I want you to find a professional counselor AND a trusted member of your program's faculty to speak to on this topic before you make a final decision. After all, this decision will have a monumental impact on your life, regardless of whether you press on or decide to leave. Still, there are circumstances in life that might warrant deciding to stop your doctoral studies.

Your health is at the top of the list of reasons you may wish to walk away. If you are battling a life-threatening illness or a chronic condition, you might decide to press on, pause, or stop your doctoral work altogether. Decisions that you will have to come to with your family may revolve around these questions: (1) "Can my body, mind, and spirit withstand the pressures of medical treatment and doctoral work simultaneously?" (2) "Are my time and energy better spent on other things or with people in my family?" (3) "Given what I am experiencing with my health, have my priorities shifted?" (4) "To what degree is this doctoral dissertation and the degree that comes with it a priority for me anymore?" If you are experiencing something of this nature, I first want you to know that I am thinking of you, I'm praying to my God for your healing, and I will do anything in my power to help you if you email me. Most importantly, I want to issue you the license to walk away *if that is what you, your family, and your trusted advisors* want. There is no shame, *none*, in making a decision that it's in your best interest to not continue your doctoral studies, provided that it is your well-thought-out decision and that you truly believe (as much as you can) that regret will not haunt you. In fact, that's what I want for you most: to not be haunted, to experience peace with any decision you make.

Your family may need you more than will allow for dissertation writing. The question you have to ask yourself is, "Does this situation warrant pausing my writing, taking a leave of absence, or canceling my doctoral work altogether?" The thought process may be quite similar to that if you were facing a health concern. Regret is something to always consider. In my mind, my family is always first; the safety, security, and thriving of my bride and my children come right after my own health. Without my family, I'm not much. There have been times when I have had to pause projects or leave them entirely behind to be there for my family; the same is probably true for you. Still, don't make such a decision in isolation. Speak with your family and your trusted advisors about what you are planning to do — this way, no one gets to live with regret around your decision. If you are leaving your doctoral studies to save your marriage, tell your spouse that you are thinking about this; talk to your couples therapist about this decision. Stopping your writing may be the best decision you have ever made, or it could haunt you, but at the very least, you want to make the decision firmly with others in your life. You are not alone, even when it feels like you are.

If you find yourself at a decision point around whether or not to continue your dissertation work, I encourage you to put down your writing for a set period of time (like four weeks). Make the conscious decision that you are going to take a short leave of absence (even if unofficially). Gather your supports around you. Whether or not you have supports, call up a therapist and meet with him or her for a few sessions. Never make this decision alone and in isolation; alone is the breeding ground for regret — and I beg you with all my heart, please save yourself from regret.

63

WHAT'S BEYOND THE THRESHOLD?

Often, I'll ask a room full of doctoral students, "What if you had your dissertation finished today; what then?" Each day, I wake up early in the morning and sip my coffee on my couch looking out over the trees behind our home. I watch the sun come up and usually dedicate at least a few minutes to thinking about what I hope will come of the day, where I and my family are headed, and what I hope the next season will hold. The visual of where my family and I are headed with one another is a powerful influence in my day. Using a few Pinterest® boards, I've collected thousands of images of where my family is headed and what I hope to create for them each day and in the future. Every time I get lost, I have a vision on which I can call. You too have dreams that are calling to you from beyond that doorway called "graduation." You have dreams about those you want to serve. You have dreams about what you want to be or what you want to accomplish. You have dreams about times with yourself, with your family, with your peers, and with those who will benefit from your hard work. You have dreams about vacations. You crave, perhaps, a time when the writing has ended. All of this you can fairly clearly imagine in your brain. However, even if you can see everything you want to have, be, and do in your future, do know that's only part of your story.

There is a hidden part of yourself that is beckoning you from beyond that doorway, a part of yourself that you cannot yet see. There is a future in front of you that is beyond your capability of seeing right now, not just because you are not a fortune teller but because you are becoming someone more and more each day. That you

— that *you* who lives in the future at some level — is lurking in the wings of that brain of yours. This part of you might be speaking to you in dreams, in the subtlest of ways, or solely through your intuition. This is not a metaphysical phenomenon; this is how our brains operate. Often, we are becoming someone more and more each day without even realizing it. While you can make some big guesses about what you are going to do post-graduation and some of the opportunities that may arise for you, you can't see the whole picture. As you are working on your dissertation, as you are putting the finishing touches on collecting your data, presenting your findings, and making some conclusions, pay special attention to that little but growing voice inside of you. Shortly, that voice is going to have much more room to speak to you. Over time, that hidden you is going to be very much in the world. As things begin to come to a triumphant conclusion for you, Dissertation Warrior, I hope that you are able to hear that voice calling to you. What kind of things might it be saying?

I am confident that this voice will be speaking to you more and more about "gratitude" as your dissertation work comes to a close: gratitude for having the chance to pursue this degree in the first place; gratitude that you had the life circumstances to be able to pursue and finish a doctoral degree; gratitude toward your family, peers, and workplace that were able to support you (or your ability to conquer in spite of these, though I hope that's not the case); and gratitude that this path is finally ending, opening to a whole new world of possibility for you and those you love. Further, you might feel a great deal of gratitude for your strength that allowed you to come this far. I so want you to feel that strength within you. I want you to acknowledge that you have done something that very few people on the planet will ever do. That should make you incredibly grateful for both your strength as a human and for the charmed circumstances in your life that allowed you to pursue this undertaking.

Strangely enough, I also know that you'll probably feel a sense of sadness too. Experienced meditators, ones who engage in regular practice, will tell you that they often develop a tenderness regarding life, themselves, and those around them. Often, I experience this as this state of, "The party is great and I don't want it to end, and yet I know that every party is going to end and that one day I am going to end too." Believe me, as one who has breathed much life into many creative projects, few great feats of exertion, like a dissertation, don't come with at least a twinge of sadness and loss. I encourage you, as you begin to feel the passing of your old life into this new phase of *you*, to pay attention to those longings that are brewing within your heart. You might laugh reading this, thinking, "I'm not going to miss any of this at all!" However, my experience working with lots of doctoral candidates has shown me that it's common to feel the loss of an era of life coming to a close. Just as your accomplishment needs to be celebrated and your new life needs to be welcomed with open eyes and arms, you need to properly lay to rest that part of your life that is coming to a close. Ask yourself, "When I cross that stage at graduation and am awarded my degree, what will I be leaving behind? Is there anything to which I need to attend before I am ready to take that walk? Can I say that I am leaving no regrets behind? Who do I need to thank as this part of my life comes to a close? Who or what do I need to leave behind? To what degree can I leave all these fears behind that plagued me during this process? What have I learned in these past years? What do I want to communicate to those around me as I gracefully yet triumphantly finish? Who do I want to be as a human being as I become a 'doctor' and graduate? In what posture do I want to be walking through this final gate? Can I walk forward with eyes and arms open, ready for what may come and with a great deal of gratitude and humility?" Walk through that final threshold unchained to regret. Go and be free.

Goodbye...

64

A FINAL WORD

Writing this book for you has been one of the greatest pleasures of my life. Each morning, know that I am thinking of you, am praying for you, and am holding you and your family in my heart. I don't say any of that lightly; I really mean it. I want to thank you for purchasing this book; you have supported my family this year during a major period of transition — a year where our dreams came to fruition in a huge way. You are supporting my children's ability to attend to a quality school. You are putting food on my table. You are keeping the electricity turned on. You allowed us to move from an unsafe neighborhood to a house safely among the trees. You changed the course of my children's lives because you picked up this book, joined one of my online trainings, or told others in your life about me. For all of these things, I find myself deeply moved by your generosity, your drive, and your desire to bring about great things in your life and for your family. Your bravery has put bread on my family's table. On top of that, you helped me fulfill my purpose on this planet by allowing me to help you fulfill yours. I feel no greater happiness than when I know that I have fulfilled my life's calling. Thank you for allowing me to live out my calling with you through these few hundred pages.

In ancient times, priests would issue a benediction to those they served. I want to leave you with these parting words as if they were the last that I might ever have a chance to speak to you:

Time is so precious. Today is so precious. "Right now" is so precious. Live out this moment and each moment you can as the best of yourself. May you be enabled to serve others in the highest capacity possible. May your daily efforts allow you to, more and more, be the servant in the world you are destined to become.

The world needs you. Finish today's good work so that you can go and do even better work tomorrow for all of those who are waiting for you beyond the Threshold.

—Guy E. White, Ed.D., June 19, 2017

Photo by Jen Downer

GUY E. WHITE, ED.D.

ABOUT THE AUTHOR

"Dr. Guy" is a Portland-based teacher, professor, and highly sought-after international public speaker. He's the author of five books, including this one. He's the creator of the most comprehensive online step-by-step dissertation writing training programs in the world: The Dissertation Mentor® Accelerator Program, The Dissertation Mentor® Home Study Course, and The Dissertation Mentor® One-To-One Mentorship.

Dr. Guy is a National Board Certified Teacher® by the National Board of Professional Teaching Standards and a certified Integral Master Coach™ by Integral Coaching Canada, both "gold standard" accreditations in the teaching and coaching fields, respectively.

Integral Master Coach™ is a registered trademark in Canada owned by Integral Coaching Canada Inc. and licensed to Guy E. White. National Board Certified Teacher® is a registered trademark of the National Board for Professional Teaching Standards and is used herein with permission.

www.TheDissertationMentor.com

THANK YOU BACKERS

Sending my warmest, most heartfelt thanks to the following people who believed in and backed my project even before I fully understood what this book would become.

Joan Harwood

Kristen White

Stefan Kolimechkov • Mustapha Hamat • Fawzi Bawab • Hilary Kouhana

Blake Clifford Sr. • Jim Simonson • Hong Quoc Nguyen
Melissa Dandy Walker • Shed Hollaway • Paul McMurray

William C. Gyldensten • Teresa J. Wilson • Simon Roberts • Franklin • Yerkhan Mindetbay
Hamdan Omar • John Burton • Kylie Meyer • Einstein Gautama

Jeff Burke • Andrea DeCosmo • Christopher Schuyler • Catalina Munguia Maguy Yancey
Laurence Bell Hammad Haq • Shawn Ta • Todd • Noemi Molina • Abdullah M. Wali-Uddin
Jeannine Lisitski • Beulah Hale • Ariann Nassel • Natalie Carter Johnson

Misty McIntyre Goodsell • Riyad • Fabian Gärtner • Fakhir Bantan • Stefano Giudici • Leisa Tucker
Rebecca Strawn • Bruce Blackshaw • Leo Mora Jr. • Cynde Wadley • Ahmad Jamal Shehadeh Kiswani
Erik Maldonado Ascanio • Ellen Maasdorp • Kerri Nugent • Lydia • Brian J. Malott

Get More Free Training from Dr. Guy

www.TheDissertationMentor.com

BACK MATTER

Don't read this book if you want a quick and dirty way to finish your dissertation or thesis, write it in a weekend, or pay someone else to write it for you. This book is for the doctoral student who wants to become the best version of himself or herself; whose doctoral journey is a quest of epic personal, professional, and spiritual transformation; and who wants to finish his or her dissertation as well. Inside this book, you'll learn, among many other things:

> › The secrets of time travel;
> › That 99% of that which gets your focus is not worth your time;
> › That "writing" your dissertation is the last thing that you should do; and
> › How to conquer your introduction, create alignment, build the best darned literature review you possibly can, find and collect your data, and connect all the clues better than a hat-wearing movie archeologist

…all while becoming a better spouse, sibling, child of your parents, and man (or woman) of all seasons.

This book is written by me, Dr. Guy. I teach, at the time of writing this book, the world's most comprehensive online step-by-step dissertation writing course. Through my online training videos, The Dissertation Mentor® Accelerator Program, The Dissertation Mentor® Home Study Course, and The Dissertation Mentor® One-To-One Mentorship, I have helped thousands of doctoral students make progress in their dissertations. I can probably help you too! This book is my manifesto about all things "doctoral."

66784938R10167

Made in the USA
Columbia, SC
19 July 2019